Gretchen Bitterlin
Dennis Johnson
Donna Price
Sylvia Ramirez
K. Lynn Savage, Series Editor

Ventures BASIC

WORKBOOK

with **Kathleen Olson**

CAMBRIDGE
UNIVERSITY PRESS

CAMBRIDGE UNIVERSITY PRESS
Cambridge, New York, Melbourne, Madrid, Cape Town, Singapore,
São Paulo, Delhi, Dubai, Tokyo, Mexico City

Cambridge University Press
32 Avenue of the Americas, New York, NY 10013–2473, USA

www.cambridge.org
Information on this title: www.cambridge.org/9780521719834

First published 2008
8th printing 2010

Printed in the United States of America

A catalog record for this publication is available from the British Library.

ISBN 978-0-521-71982-7 pack consisting of Student's Book and Audio CD
ISBN 978-0-521-71983-4 Workbook
ISBN 978-0-521-71987-2 Literacy Workbook
ISBN 978-0-521-71986-5 pack consisting of Teacher's Edition and Teacher's Toolkit Audio CD / CD-ROM
ISBN 978-0-521-71984-1 CDs (Audio)
ISBN 978-0-521-71985-8 Cassettes

Art direction, book design, photo research, and layout services: Adventure House, NYC

Contents

Welcome

1 Write the letters.

A B C *D* E F
G H I J K L
M N O P Q R
S T U V W X
Y Z

2 Write the letters.

a b c d e f
g h i j k l
m n o p q r
s t u v w x
y z

Check your answers. See page 130.

3 Look at the pictures. Write the letters. Then write the words.

1

$\underline{W}$ r i t e.

_____*Write*_____ .

2

___ o i n t.

_____ .

3

___ e a d.

_____ .

4

___ i s t e n.

_____ .

5

___ i r c l e.

_____ .

6

___ a t c h.

_____ .

Check your answers. See page 130.

4 Write the numbers.

1	**2**	**3**	*4*	**5**
6	*7*	**8**	**9**	*10*
11	**12**	*13*	**14**	**15**
16	**17**	**18**	*19*	**20**

5 Write the numbers.

one	**two**	*three*
four	*five*	**six**
seven	**eight**	*nine*
ten	**eleven**	*twelve*
thirteen	*fourteen*	**fifteen**
sixteen	**seventeen**	*eighteen*
nineteen	*twenty*	

Check your answers. See page 130.

6 Look at the pictures. Write the numbers.

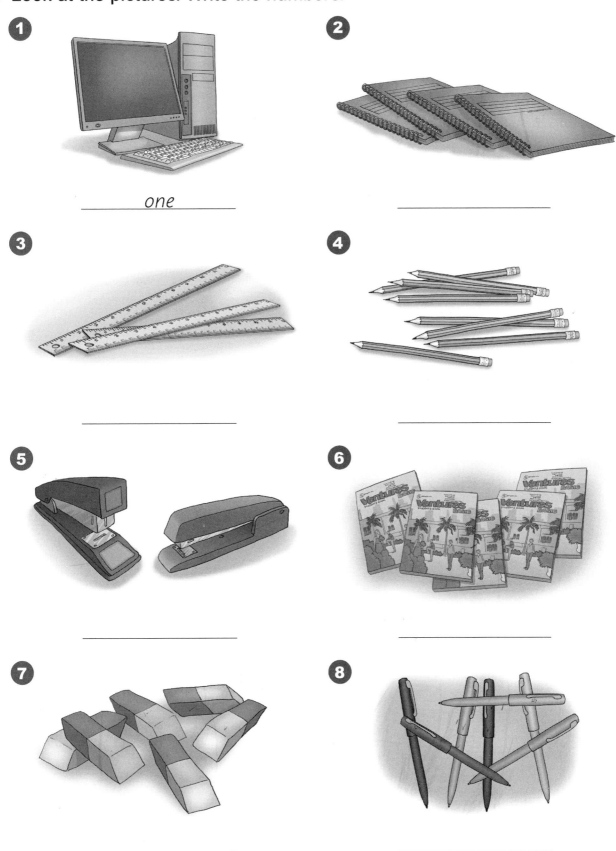

1 _____ *one* _____

2 _____

3 _____

4 _____

5 _____

6 _____

7 _____

8 _____

Check your answers. See page 130.

Lesson **A** Get ready

1 Look at the ID card. Write the words.

Student ID Card

1 Anna   2 Lopez
first name   last name

3 Mexico
country

4 254   5 555-2992
area code   phone number

1. _f i r s t   n a m e_
2. __ __ __ __   __ __ __ __
3. __ __ __ __ __ __ __
4. __ __ __ __   __ __ __ __
5. __ __ __ __   __ __ __ __ __ __

2 Write the words from Exercise 1.

1. | A | n | n | a |

   first name

2. ☐ ☐ ☐ ☐

   last name

3. ☐ ☐ ☐ ☐ ☐ ☐

   country

4. ☐ ☐ ☐

   area code

5. ☐ ☐ ☐ - ☐ ☐ ☐ ☐

   phone number

Check your answers. See page 130.

3 Match.

1. last ——— card
2. first   code
3. phone   name
4. area   number
5. ID   name

4 Write the words.

area code	first name	last name	phone number

1. (917) 555-4980   _phone number_
2. (917) 555-4980   _____
3. John Smith   _____
4. John Smith   _____

5 Write the words.

area code	first name	last name	phone number

1. _first name_

3. _____

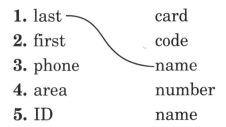

J JOHNSON – JONES

Craig Johnson . . . . . (786) 555-0874

Vera Johnson . . . . . . (385) 555-1232

2. _____

4. _____

Check your answers. See page 130.

1 Look at the picture. Match. Write the letter.

| Lorena | Kalifa | Fabio | Shen | Yuri | Diane |

1. _f_ Diane   a. Brazil
2. ___ Fabio   b. China
3. ___ Kalifa   c. Mexico
4. ___ Lorena   d. Russia
5. ___ Shen   e. Somalia
6. ___ Yuri   f. the United States

2 Unscramble the letters. Write the countries.

1. C n a h i   _____China_____
2. z i l B a r   _____
3. s s i a R u   _____
4. e x M i o c   _____
5. o m S l i a a   _____

Check your answers. See page 130.

3 Look at the picture. Write the countries.

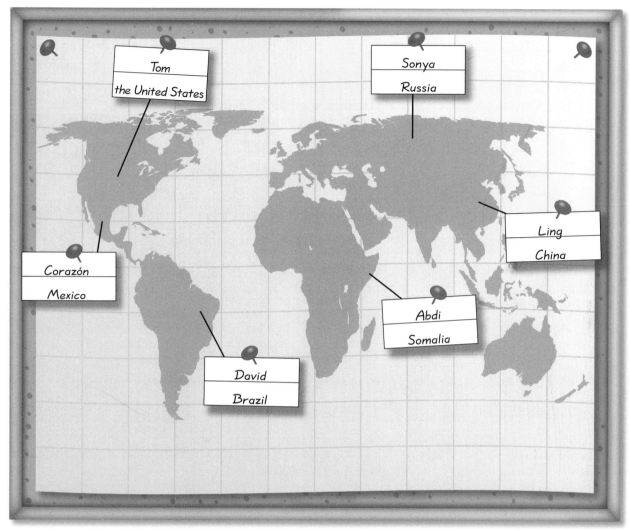

1. Where is Abdi from?   _____Somalia_____ .
2. Where is Tom from?   _____ .
3. Where is Ling from?   _____ .
4. Where is David from?   _____ .
5. Where is Sonya from?   _____ .
6. Where is Corazón from? _____ .

Check your answers. See page 130.

What's your name?

Study the chart on page 126.

1 Look at the cards. Write *his* or *her*.

1. A What's _____*her*_____ first name?
   B Louise.

2. A What's _____ last name?
   B Ramirez.

3. A What's _____ area code?
   B 614.

4. A What's _____ phone number?
   B 555-9770.

5. A What's _____ area code?
   B 825.

6. A What's _____ first name?
   B Carlos.

7. A What's _____ last name?
   B Miller.

8. A What's _____ phone number?
   B 555-8052.

Check your answers. See page 130.

2 Write *My* or *your*.

Alan What's _____*your*_____ first name?
₁

Manuel _____ first name is Manuel.
₂

Alan What's _____ last name?
₃

Manuel _____ last name is Alvez.
₄

Alan What's _____ area code?
₅

Manuel _____ area code is 917.
₆

Alan What's _____ phone number?
₇

Manuel _____ phone number is 555-9845.
₈

3 Complete the form about Manuel.

Job Interview Notes

First name: _____*Manuel*_____

Last name: _____

Area code: _____

Phone number: _____

Check your answers. See page 130.

1 Circle the answers.

Hello

First name	Boris
Last name	Egorov
Country	Russia

1. His name is ___ .   (Boris Egorov)   Egorov Boris
2. His last name is ___ .   Boris   Egorov
3. His first name is ___ .   Boris   Egorov
4. He is from ___ .   Russia   country

2 Match. Write the letter.

Pamela
First name

Reese
Last name

Canada
Country

1. _c_ What's her name?   a. Reese
2. ___ What's her last name?   b. Canada
3. ___ What's her first name?   c. Pamela Reese
4. ___ Where is she from?   d. Pamela

Check your answers. See page 130.

3 Complete the calendar.

JANUARY					
	1	2	3	4	5
6	7	8	9	10	11	12
13	14	15	16	17	18	19
20	21	22	23	24	25	26
27	28	29	30	31		

February

					1	2
3	4	5	6	7	8	9
10	11	12	13	14	15	16
17	18	19	20	21	22	23
24	25	26	27	28	29	

_____

						1
2	3	4	5	6	7	8
9	10	11	12	13	14	15
16	17	18	19	20	21	22
23	24	25	26	27	28	29
30	31					

APRIL					
	1	2	3	4	5
6	7	8	9	10	11	12
13	14	15	16	17	18	19
20	21	22	23	24	25	26
27	28	29	30			

_____

				1	2	3
4	5	6	7	8	9	10
11	12	13	14	15	16	17
18	19	20	21	22	23	24
25	26	27	28	29	30	31

_____

1	2	3	4	5	6	7
8	9	10	11	12	13	14
15	16	17	18	19	20	21
22	23	24	25	26	27	28
29	30					

JULY					
	1	2	3	4	5
6	7	8	9	10	11	12
13	14	15	16	17	18	19
20	21	22	23	24	25	26
27	28	29	30	31		

_____

					1	2
3	4	5	6	7	8	9
10	11	12	13	14	15	16
17	18	19	20	21	22	23
24	25	26	27	28	29	30
31						

_____

1	2	3	4	5	6	
7	8	9	10	11	12	13
14	15	16	17	18	19	20
21	22	23	24	25	26	27
28	29	30				

OCTOBER					
		1	2	3	4
5	6	7	8	9	10	11
12	13	14	15	16	17	18
19	20	21	22	23	24	25
26	27	28	29	30	31	

_____

						1
2	3	4	5	6	7	8
9	10	11	12	13	14	15
16	17	18	19	20	21	22
23	24	25	26	27	28	29
30						

DECEMBER					
	1	2	3	4	5	6
7	8	9	10	11	12	13
14	15	16	17	18	19	20
21	22	23	24	25	26	27
28	29	30	31			

4 Read. Write the answers.

Birthdays in Group 1

January: Lynn   April: Tony
February: Diego   June: Jim
July: Tina

1. When is Jim's birthday?   *In June* .
2. When is Lynn's birthday? _____ .
3. When is Diego's birthday? _____ .
4. When is Tony's birthday? _____ .
5. When is Tina's birthday? _____ .

Check your answers. See page 130.

Lesson E *Writing*

1 Complete the words.

area code	country	first name	last name	phone number

1. c <u>o u n t r y</u>

2. a __ __ __   c __ __ __

3. f __ __ __ __   n __ __ __

4. l __ __ __   n __ __ __

5. p __ __ __ __   n __ __ __ __ __

2 Look at the ID card. Complete the sentences.

1. Her ____*first*____ ____*name*____ is Mei.

2. Her _____ _____ is Wu.

3. Her _____ _____ is 773.

4. Her _____ _____ is 555-1173.

5. She is from _____ .

Check your answers. See page 130.

14 Unit 1

3 Look at the ID card. Complete the sentences.

Springfield Library

Emma
First name

Harris
Last name

(407)
Area code

555-6524
Phone number

1. Her first name is _____ Emma _____ .

2. Her last name is _____ .

3. Her area code is _____ .

4. Her phone number is _____ .

4 Read. Complete the driver's license.

Meet the new student at River Valley Driving School. His first name is Octavio. His last name is Diaz. He is from Mexico. His area code is 206. His phone number is 555-3687. His birthday is December 7, 1990.

INTERNATIONAL
DRIVER'S LICENSE

Octavio
First name

_____
Last name

_____
Date of birth (birthday)

_____
Place of birth (country)

_____
Area code

_____
Phone number

Check your answers. See page 130.

Another view

1 Read the sentences. Look at the form. Circle the answers.

> ## Adult English Program
> ## Registration Form
> September 2008
>
> **Name:** _Camila Silva_
>
> **Address:** _2000 Chicago Avenue_
>
> _Oak Park, IL 60304_
>
> **Phone:** _(708) 555-1979_
>
> **Birthday:** _October 16, 1987_
>
> **Country:** _Brazil_
>
> **Signature:** _Camila Silva_

1. Her last name is ___ .
a. Camila
(b.) Silva

2. Her area code is ___ .
a. 60304
b. 708

3. She is from ___ .
a. Brazil
b. Chicago Avenue

4. Her first name is ___ .
a. Camila
b. Silva

5. Her phone number is ___ .
a. 555-1987
b. 555-1979

6. Her birthday is in ___ .
a. September
b. October

Check your answers. See page 130.

2 Circle the words.

1. **country**   c o (c o u n t r y) t e
2. **name**   m e n a m e a n
3. **June**   l J u l J u n e J y
4. **month**   m o n m o n t h t h
5. **birthday** d a y b i r t h d a y b i
6. **phone**   p h p h o n e p n

3 What is different? Cross it out.

1.	**Brazil**	China	~~August~~	Mexico
2.	**470**	555-9832	212	201
3.	**555-6782**	555-1508	555-3744	972
4.	**March**	Somalia	October	July
5.	**Vladimir**	William	Russia	Rachel
6.	**China**	January	Mexico	Somalia
7.	**May**	September	December	Brazil

4 Number the months in the correct order.

_1_ January   ___ December
___ April   ___ March
___ August   ___ February
___ July   ___ October
___ May   ___ September
___ November   ___ June

January

Sunday	Monday	Tuesday	Wednesday	Thursday	Friday	Saturday
	1	2	3	4	5	6
7	8	9	10	11	12	13
14	15	16	17	18	19	20
21	22	23	24	25	26	27
28	29	30	31			

Check your answers. See page 131.

Lesson **A** *Get ready*

At school

1 Look at the pictures. Match.

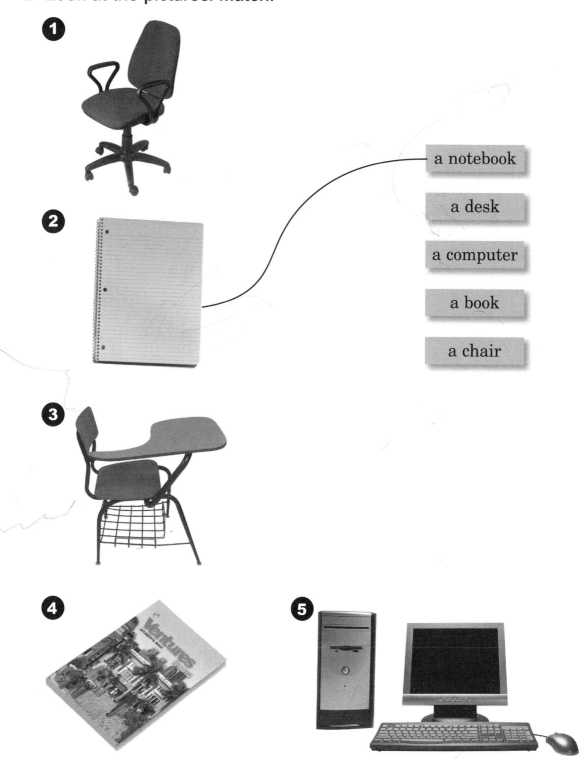

1

2

a notebook

a desk

a computer

a book

a chair

3

4

5

Check your answers. See page 131.

2 Look at the picture. What do you see? Check (✓).

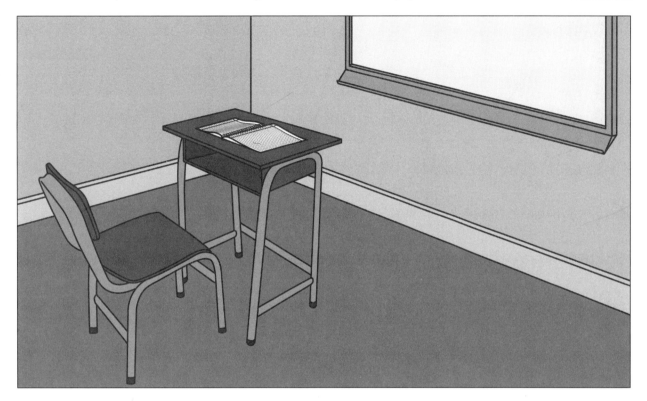

☑ a notebook
☐ a pencil
☐ a chair
☐ a desk
☐ a computer
☐ a book

3 Complete the words.

1. b o o *k*
2. n o t e b o o ___
3. d e s ___
4. ___ o m p u t e r
5. p e n ___ i l
6. ___ h a i r

Check your answers. See page 131.

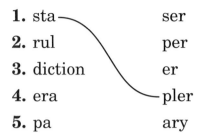

Classroom objects

1 Match.

1. sta ——————— ser
2. rul —————————— per
3. diction ————— er
4. era ——————— pler
5. pa ————————— ary

2 Find the words.

dictionary	eraser	paper	pen	ruler	stapler

d	i	c	t	i	o	n	a	r	y
p	i	n	d	e	r	a	s	e	r
l	a	e	s	t	a	p	l	e	r
p	a	p	e	r	b	v	z	p	x
w	s	b	a	l	o	y	p	e	n
q	u	y	s	f	r	u	l	e	r

Check your answers. See page 131.

3 Complete the words.

dictionary	eraser	paper	pen	ruler	stapler

1. d _i_ _c_ _t_ _i_ _o_ _n_ _a_ _r_ _y_
2. p __ __ __ __
3. p __ __
4. r __ __ __ __
5. s __ __ __ __ __ __
6. e __ __ __ __ __

4 Look at the pictures. Write the words.

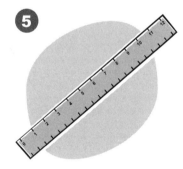

1. a _____ pen _____
2. a _____
3. an _____
4. a _____
5. a _____
6. _____

Check your answers. See page 131.

Where's my pencil?

1 Look at the picture. Match. Write the letter.

1. _c_ pencil   a. on the desk
2. ___ eraser   b. on the floor
3. ___ paper   c. in the desk
4. ___ dictionary   d. on the chair
5. ___ notebook   e. on the notebook

2 Look at the picture in Exercise 1. Write *In* or *On*.

1. Where's my pencil?   _____*In*_____ the desk.
2. Where's my notebook?   _____ the chair.
3. Where's my dictionary?   _____ the floor.
4. Where's my paper?   _____ the desk.
5. Where's my eraser?   _____ the notebook.

Check your answers. See page 131.

3 Look at the picture. Write the answers.

1. **A** Where's my dictionary?

   B *On the desk* _____ .

2. **A** Where's my pencil?

   B _____ .

3. **A** Where's my eraser?

   B _____ .

4. **A** Where's my paper?

   B _____ .

5. **A** Where's my notebook?

   B _____ .

6. **A** Where's my ruler?

   B _____ .

Check your answers. See page 131.

Lesson D **Reading**

1 Circle the words.

1. **notebook**   n o t (n o t e b o o k) t e
2. **eraser**   e r e r a s e r a s
3. **computer**   c c o m p u t e r t e r
4. **pencil**   e n p e n c i l i l p
5. **desk**   e s k d e s k d e n c i l
6. **book**   k o b o o o k b o o k

2 Read. Circle the correct sentences.

Dear Students,

Welcome to English class!
- You need a pencil.
- You need an eraser.
- You need a notebook.
- You need a dictionary.
- You need a ruler.

Thank you.

Your teacher,
Ellen

CENTER AVENUE ADULT SCHOOL

1. (You need a dictionary.)   You need a chair.
2. You need paper.   You need a pencil.
3. You need a computer.   You need a notebook.
4. You need a ruler.   You need a stapler.
5. You need an eraser.   You need a pen.

Check your answers. See page 131.

3 Number the days in the correct order.

___ Sunday

___ Friday

_1_ Monday

___ Wednesday

___ Thursday

___ Tuesday

___ Saturday

4 Write the words.

Friday	Monday	Sunday	Thursday	Tuesday	Wednesday

S _u_ _n_ _d_ _a_ _y_

M __ __ __ a __

t

__ u __ __ __ __ __

__ r __ __ __ __

__ __ d __ __ __ __ __ __

a

T __ __ __ __ __ __ y

5 Write the days of the week.

A What day is it?

B _Friday_ .

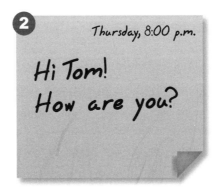

Thursday, 8:00 p.m.

Hi Tom!
How are you?

A What day is it?

B _____ .

Tuesday, August 20

Dear Mom,

I miss you!

Love, Mary

postcard

A What day is it?

B _____ .

Check your answers. See page 131.

1 Look at the picture. Complete the sentences.

dictionary	eraser	notebook	pencil	ruler

1. The _____notebook_____ is on the floor.

2. The _____ is on the chair.

3. The _____ is on the table.

4. The _____ is on the notebook.

5. The _____ is in the notebook.

Check your answers. See page 131.

2 Look at the picture. Write *in* or *on*.

What a mess! The dictionary is __*on*__ the chair. The stapler
                                  1

is _____ the dictionary. The eraser is _____ the desk. The pencil
     2   3

is _____ the desk. The notebook is _____ the floor. And the ruler
     4   5

is _____ the notebook.
     6

3 Unscramble the letters. Match.

1. c i p e l n   ruler

2. r a e r s e   notebook

3. u l r e r   dictionary

4. a p p r e   pencil

5. a r y d t c i o i n   eraser

6. t o o b k e n o   paper

4 Write the words from Exercise 3.

School Supplies for Class

1. I need a _____ *pencil* _____ .
2. I need an _____ .
3. I need a _____ .
4. I need _____ .
5. I need a _____ .
6. I need a _____ .

Check your answers. See page 131.

Another view

1 Read the sentences. Look at the class schedule. Circle the answers.

Red Rock Adult School Classes

Monday	Tuesday	Wednesday	Thursday
Computers	English	Computers	English
7:00–8:30 p.m.	6:30–8:00 p.m.	7:00–8:30 p.m.	6:30–8:00 p.m.

Computer Teacher:	English Teacher:
Sheila Brown	Brad Ryan
Room: 106	**Room:** 217

1. English class is on ___ .
   a. Monday and Wednesday
   b. Tuesday and Thursday *(circled)*

2. Computer class is on ___ .
   a. Tuesday and Wednesday
   b. Monday and Wednesday

3. Computer class is in ___ .
   a. Room 106
   b. Room 217

4. The teacher on Monday and Wednesday is ___ .
   a. Brad Ryan
   b. Sheila Brown

5. The teacher on Tuesday and Thursday is ___ .
   a. Brad Ryan
   b. Sheila Brown

Check your answers. See page 131.

2 Complete the puzzle.

desk	dictionary	eraser	notebook	pen	pencil	ruler	stapler

Across →

1

4

5
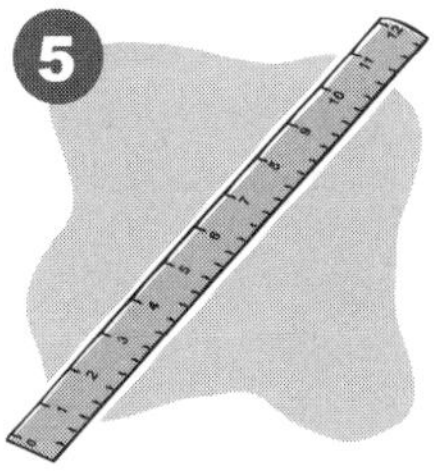

7

8

Down ↓

2

3

6

Check your answers. See page 131.

Get ready

1 Look at the pictures. Circle the answers.

son (grandmother)

daughter   son

grandfather   daughter

father   mother

father   grandmother

mother   son

2 Complete the words.

1. s _o_ n

2. f __ t h __ r

3. m __ t h __ r

4. g r __ n d m __ t h __ r

5. d __ __ g h t __ r

6. g r __ n d f __ t h __ r

Check your answers. See page 132.

3 Look at the picture. What do you see? Check (✓).

☑ father   ☐ grandmother
☐ grandfather   ☐ son
☐ daughter   ☐ mother

4 Look at the picture in Exercise 3. Write the words.

1. _f_ _a_ _t_ _h_ _e_ _r_
2. __ __ __ __ __ __
3. __ __ __ __ __ __ __ __ __ __ __
4. __ __ __ __ __ __ __ __ __ __ __
5. __ __ __ __ __ __ __ __

Check your answers. See page 132.

1 Match.

1. sister   daughter
2. son   uncle
3. grandmother   brother
4. husband   father
5. mother   grandfather
6. aunt   wife

2 Write the words.

aunt	brother	husband	sister	wife

```
        m
   b  r  o  t  h  e  r
  __ __ __ t
           h __ __ __ __ __ __
  __ __ __ e
__ __ __ __ __ r
```

Check your answers. See page 132.

3 Circle the correct pictures of Michael's family.

1. aunt and uncle **(a)** Anita Rick   **b** Michael Emily

2. mother and father **a** Julie Jason   **b** Michael Emily

3. brother and sister **a** Julie Jason   **b** Michael Emily

4 Look at the pictures in Exercise 3. Write the answers.

1. **A** Who is Michael?
   B Emily's _____*brother*_____ .

2. **A** Who is Emily?
   B Michael's _____ .

3. **A** Who is Jason?
   B Michael's _____ .

4. **A** Who is Julie?
   B Michael's _____ .

5. **A** Who is Rick?
   B Michael's _____ .

Check your answers. See page 132.

Lesson C *Do you have a sister?*

Study the chart on page 126.

1 Look at the pictures. Circle the answers. Then write the answers.

A Do you have a son?
B *No, we don't.*
       Yes, we do. (No, we don't.)

A Do you have a brother?
B _____
       Yes, I do. No, I don't.

A Do you have a daughter?
B _____
       Yes, we do. No, we don't.

A Do you have a wife?
B _____
       Yes, I do. No, I don't.

A Do you have a grandmother?
B _____
       Yes, I do. No, I don't.

Check your answers. See page 132.

2 Look at the picture of Carla's family. Write the words.

daughter	husband	sister	son

1. A Carla, do you have a _____ *sister* _____ ?
B Yes, I do.
A What's her name?
B Gabriela.

2. A Carla, do you have a _____ ?
B Yes, I do.
A What's her name?
B Inez.

3. A Carla, do you have a _____ ?
B Yes, I do.
A What's his name?
B Roberto.

4. A Carla, do you have a _____ ?
B Yes, I do.
A What's his name?
B Alfredo.

Check your answers. See page 132.

1 Read. Write the words.

My Family

My name is Geraldo. This is my family.
This is my father. His name is Hugo. This is
my mother. Her name is Magdalena. This is
my wife, Pilar. This is my daughter, Ramona.

| daughter | father | mother | wife |

1. _____wife_____

2. _____

3. _____

4. _____

Geraldo

Ramona

Hugo

Pilar

Magdalena

2 Look at the story in Exercise 1. Circle the answers.

1. Ramona is Geraldo's mother.   Yes   (No)
2. Pilar is Geraldo's wife.   Yes   No
3. Magdalena is Geraldo's mother.   Yes   No
4. Hugo is Geraldo's brother.   Yes   No
5. Ramona is Hugo's wife.   Yes   No

Check your answers. See page 132.

3 Complete the chart.

baby	boy	girl	man	teenager	woman

Male	Female	Male or Female
boy		

4 Circle the answers. Then write the answers.

1. Pat is a mother. Pat is a _____woman_____ .
man (woman)

2. Joe is a father. Joe is a _____ .
man   woman

3. Charles is a son. Charles is a _____ .
boy   girl

4. Debbie is a daughter. Debbie is a _____ .
boy   girl

5. Sharon is a wife. Sharon is a _____ .
man   woman

6. Jimmy is a husband. Jimmy is a _____ .
man   woman

7. Nancy is a grandmother. Nancy is a _____ .
man   woman

8. Heather is 13 years old. Heather is a _____ .
teenager   baby

9. Mark is one year old. Mark is a _____ .
teenager   baby

Check your answers. See page 132.

1 Unscramble the letters. Write the words.

daughter	grandfather	mother	sister	uncle	wife

1. i f w e   _wife_
2. n u l e c   _____
3. s s i e t r   _____
4. o e m h t r   _____
5. d t h r e g a u   _____
6. g f r a t a d n r h e   _____

2 Write. Use the words from Exercise 1.

1. aunt and _____ _uncle_ _____
2. brother and _____
3. son and _____
4. husband and _____
5. father and _____
6. grandmother and _____

3 Look at the baby's family. Write the words.

1. _____
2. _____
3. _baby_____
4. _____
5. _____

Check your answers. See page 132.

4 Look at Viktor's family. Write the words.

| brother | daughter | father | mother | son | wife |

Greg
1. _____father_____

Irina
2. _____

Boris
3. _____

Viktor

Sylvia
4. _____

Arthur
5. _____

Olivia
6. _____

5 Look at the picture in Exercise 4. Complete the sentences.

1. Viktor is Sylvia's _____husband_____ .
2. Viktor is Irina's _____ .
3. Viktor is Arthur's _____ .
4. Viktor is Greg's _____ .
5. Viktor is Boris's _____ .
6. Viktor is Olivia's _____ .

Check your answers. See page 132.

Another view

1 Read the questions. Look at the form. Circle the answers.

Census Form

Name: Tia Sanchez

Address: 333 Main Street

City: San Antonio	State: TX	Zip Code: 78205

Who lives with you in your house?

First name	Last name	Relation
1. Javier	Gonzalez	father
2. Consuela	Gonzalez	mother
3. Roberto	Sanchez	husband
4. Rodrigo	Sanchez	son
5. Pedro	Sanchez	son
6. Lara	Sanchez	daughter

1. Who is Lara Sanchez?

  a. Tia's mother.

  (b.) Tia's daughter.

2. Who is Roberto Sanchez?

  a. Tia's son.

  b. Tia's husband.

3. Who is Pedro Sanchez?

  a. Tia's son.

  b. Tia's father.

4. Who is Consuela Gonzalez?

  a. Tia's mother.

  b. Tia's daughter.

5. Who is Javier Gonzalez?

  a. Tia's son.

  b. Tia's father.

6. Who is Tia Sanchez?

  a. Roberto's wife.

  b. Roberto's mother.

Check your answers. See page 132.

2 What is different? Cross it out.

1. **aunt**	woman	~~father~~	wife
2. **grandfather**	son	husband	aunt
3. **daughter**	son	wife	grandmother
4. **brother**	uncle	aunt	man
5. **mother**	brother	grandmother	daughter
6. **father**	boy	grandfather	wife
7. **girl**	man	aunt	woman

3 Find the words.

baby	husband	mother	sister
teenager	uncle	wife	woman

w	i	f	e	o	r	d	i	m	b	a	b	y	g
o	w	o	m	a	n	r	s	i	s	t	r	v	e
s	i	s	t	e	r	s	t	f	l	c	e	l	o
c	a	m	e	r	t	m	o	t	h	e	r	n	k
h	u	s	b	a	n	d	s	h	o	u	m	k	l
n	m	o	w	i	e	t	e	e	n	a	g	e	r
u	n	c	l	e	t	b	u	b	f	w	a	p	o

Check your answers. See page 132.

Get ready

1 Look at the pictures. Circle the words.

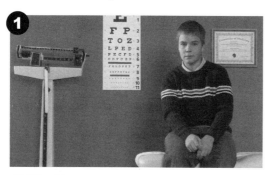

1

patient
nurse
doctor

2

nurse
doctor's office
doctor

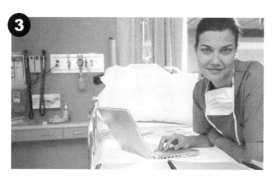

3

medicine
patient
nurse

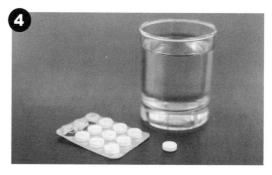

4

doctor
nurse
medicine

5

medicine
doctor
patient

6

doctor's office
nurse
patient

Check your answers. See page 132.

Health

2 Look at the picture. Write the words.

| doctor | doctor's office | medicine | nurse | patient |

1. <u>d o c t o r's   o f f i c e</u>

2. __ __ __ __ __ __

3. __ __ __ __ __

4. __ __ __ __ __ __ __

5. __ __ __ __ __ __ __ __

3 Match. Write the words.

1. med   fice   *medicine*

2. doc   tient   _____

3. pa   tor   _____

4. of   icine   _____

Check your answers. See page 132.

Parts of the body

1 Complete the words.

1. h _a_ n d   4. ___ r m

2. h e ___ d   5. l ___ g

3. f ___ o t   6. s t o m ___ c h

2 Look at the pictures. What hurts? Write the words from Exercise 1.

My ____stomach____ .

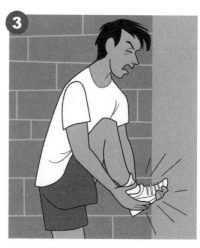

My _____ .

My _____ .

My _____ .

My _____ .

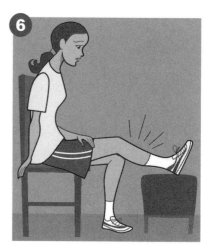

My _____ .

Check your answers. See page 132.

3 Look at the pictures. Complete the sentences.

A What's the matter?

B My _____ *foot* _____ hurts.

A What's the matter?

B My _____ hurts.

A What's the matter?

B My _____ hurts.

A What's the matter?

B My _____ hurts.

A What's the matter?

B My _____ hurts.

A What's the matter?

B My _____ hurts.

Check your answers. See page 133.

My feet hurt.

1 Match.

1. eye   feet
2. hand   arms
3. foot   heads
4. arm   eyes
5. leg   hands
6. head   legs

2 Find the words.

arms	eyes	feet	foot	hands	head	legs

```
r  e  p  l  e  g  s  t  u  r
f  q  b  o  p  h  a  n  d  s
o  u  m  j  f  e  e  t  k  e
f  o  o  t  t  l  s  c  z  j
t  e  r  h  e  a  d  z  y  e
a  r  m  s  c  o  m  u  t  r
l  e  k  f  t  p  e  y  e  s
```

Check your answers. See page 133.

3 Look at the pictures. Complete the chart.

	1	2
1. 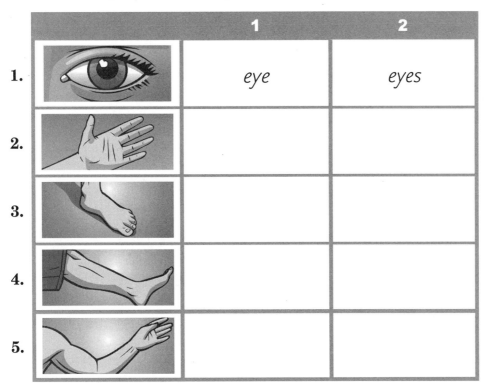	*eye*	*eyes*
2.		
3.		
4.		
5.		

4 Look at the pictures. Write the words.

A What hurts?
B My ____*legs*____ .

A What hurts?
B My _____ .

A What hurts?
B My _____ .

A What hurts?
B My _____ .

A What hurts?
B My _____ .

A What hurts?
B My _____ .

Check your answers. See page 133.

1 Look at the picture. Read. Complete the sentences.

Where's the Doctor?

Five patients are at the doctor's office. The nurse is talking to the patients. Ruth's stomach hurts. Jun's arm hurts. Liliana's leg hurts. Omar's hand hurts. Tano's foot hurts. Where's the doctor? Doctor Han is not in his office. His head hurts. He is home in bed.

1. *Nurse* What hurts?
   Ruth My ____stomach____ hurts.

2. *Nurse* What hurts?
   Omar My _____ hurts.

3. *Nurse* What hurts?
   Tano My _____ hurts.

4. *Nurse* What hurts?
   Jun My _____ hurts.

5. *Nurse* What hurts?
   Liliana My _____ hurts.

6. *Nurse* What hurts?
   Doctor My _____ hurts.

Check your answers. See page 133.

2 Look at the picture. Match. Write the letter.

Nurse's Office

| Mrs. Simon | Matt | Ella | Stefano | Reyna | Minh |

1. _c_ Mrs. Simon   a. a cold
2. ___ Matt   b. a fever
3. ___ Ella   c. a headache
4. ___ Stefano   d. a sore throat
5. ___ Reyna   e. a stomachache
6. ___ Minh   f. a toothache

3 Look at the pictures. Complete the sentences.

1

I have a
___toothache___ .

2

I have a
_____ .

3

I have a
_____ .

Check your answers. See page 133.

Writing

1 Complete the puzzle.

arm	cold	eyes	headache
legs	sore throat	stomachache	toothache

Across →

 1
 4
 5
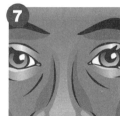 7

Down ↓

 1
 2
 3
 6

4 a r m

Check your answers. See page 133.

2 Unscramble the letters. Write the words.

| cold | headache | fever | sore throat | stomachache |

1. c l d o   _cold_
2. v r e e f   _____
3. d c h e a a e h   _____
4. o m a c s t h c e h a   _____
5. o r s e   o h r t a t   _____

3 Read. Complete the sentences.

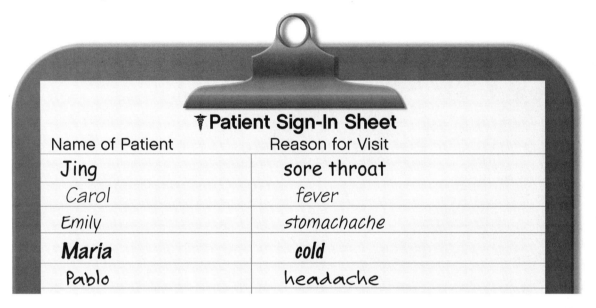

Patient Sign-In Sheet

Name of Patient	Reason for Visit
Jing	sore throat
Carol	fever
Emily	stomachache
Maria	cold
Pablo	headache

1. Jing   I have a ___ _sore throat_ ___ .
2. Maria   I have a _____ .
3. Pablo   I have a _____ .
4. Emily   I have a _____ .
5. Carol   I have a _____ .

Check your answers. See page 133.

1 Read the sentences. Look at the label. Circle the answers.

Feel better now!

Cold Cure

For relief of colds, sore throats, and fevers

50 Tablets

Do not use after January 2011.

1. This medicine is for a ___ .
   a. cold
   b. toothache

2. This medicine is for a ___ .
   a. headache
   b. fever

3. This medicine is for a ___ .
   a. stomachache
   b. sore throat

4. Do not take this medicine ___ .
   a. after January 2011
   b. after January 2010

5. This medicine has ___ .
   a. 20 tablets
   b. 50 tablets

Check your answers. See page 133.

2 Look at the picture. Write the words.

1. _____hands_____

2. _____

3. _____

4. _____

5. _____

3 Look at the picture. What hurts? Complete the sentences.

1. _____My head_____ hurts.
2. _____ hurts.
3. _____ hurts.
4. _____ hurts.

Check your answers. See page 133.

Lesson A *Get ready*

1 Look at the pictures. Match.

library

restaurant

school

supermarket

bank

Around town

Check your answers. See page 133.

2 Unscramble the letters. Write the words.

| bank | library | restaurant |
| school | street | supermarket |

1. s r e t e t   *street*

2. k a b n   _____

3. h c s l o o   _____

4. b l i r r a y   _____

5. t a u n r a t e s r   _____

6. m k t a r e p e r u s   _____

3 Complete the puzzle. Use the words from Exercise 2.

Check your answers. See page 133.

Places around town

1 Match. Then write the words.

1. drug   center   *drugstore*
2. movie   store   _____
3. senior   office   _____
4. post   theater   _____

2 Find the words.

drugstore	hospital	laundromat
movie theater	post office	senior center

h	p	o	s	h	o	s	p	i	t	a	l	i	n
n	o	x	u	l	f	n	e	c	e	t	d	y	g
o	w	e	n	t	d	r	u	g	s	t	o	r	e
r	e	p	o	s	t	o	f	f	i	c	e	l	o
c	a	s	e	n	i	o	r	c	e	n	t	e	r
e	g	z	x	u	r	i	s	h	o	u	m	k	l
n	m	o	v	i	e	t	h	e	a	t	e	r	m
l	a	n	o	l	a	u	n	d	r	o	m	a	t

Check your answers. See page 133.

3 Look at the pictures. Write the answers.

drugstore	hospital	laundromat
movie theater	post office	senior center

A Where's Mark?

B At the _____ *hospital* _____ .

A Where's Maya?

B At the _____ .

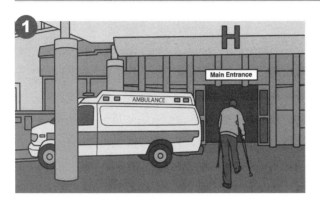

A Where's Jane?

B At the _____ .

A Where's Pavel?

B At the _____ .

A Where's Yong Suk?

B At the _____ .

A Where's Peter?

B At the _____ .

Check your answers. See page 133.

It's on Main Street.

1 Look at the picture. Circle the answers. Then write.

1. The drugstore is _____*next to*_____ the supermarket.
   (next to)   across from

2. The school is _____ the library.
   next to   across from

3. The supermarket is _____ the post office.
   next to   across from

4. The post office is _____ Main Street.
   on   across from

5. The bank is _____ the restaurant and the
   across from   between
   movie theater.

6. The restaurant is _____ the post office.
   between   across from

Check your answers. See page 133.

2 Look at the map. Write the words.

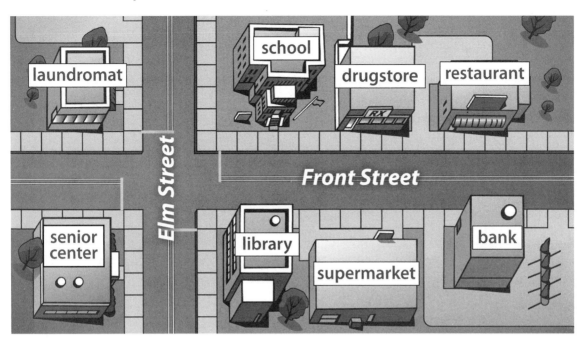

Across from	Between	Next to	On

1. **A** Where's the restaurant?
   B _Next to_____ the drugstore.

2. **A** Where's the school?
   B _____ the library.

3. **A** Where's the drugstore?
   B _____ the school and the restaurant.

4. **A** Where's the restaurant?
   B _____ Front Street.

3 Look at the map in Exercise 2. Match. Write the letter.

1. _c_ the laundromat   a. next to the drugstore
2. ___ the supermarket   b. across from the laundromat
3. ___ the school   c. on Elm Street
4. ___ the library   d. between the library and the bank
5. ___ the senior center   e. across from the school

Check your answers. See page 133.

Reading

1 Read. Complete the map.

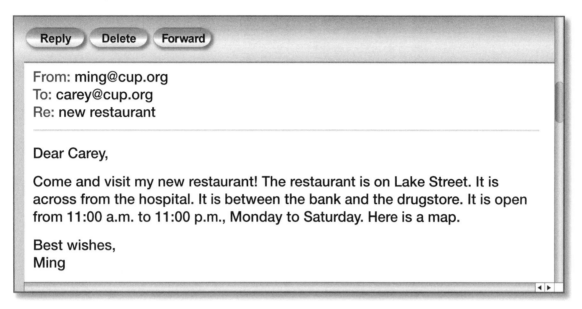

Reply   Delete   Forward

From: ming@cup.org
To: carey@cup.org
Re: new restaurant

Dear Carey,

Come and visit my new restaurant! The restaurant is on Lake Street. It is across from the hospital. It is between the bank and the drugstore. It is open from 11:00 a.m. to 11:00 p.m., Monday to Saturday. Here is a map.

Best wishes,
Ming

1. *bank*   2.   3.

LAKE STREET

4.

2 Look at your map in Exercise 1. Write the answers.

1. **A** Where's the restaurant?
   B Across from the _____*hospital*_____ .

2. **A** Where's the restaurant?
   B On _____ .

3. **A** Where's the restaurant?
   B Between the _____ and the _____ .

4. **A** Where's the bank?
   B Next to the _____ .

Check your answers. See page 134.

3 Complete the words.

bicycle	bus	car	foot	taxi	train

1. by c _a_ _r_

2. by t __ __ __

3. by b __ __ __ __ __ __

4. by b __ __

5. by t __ __ __ __

6. on f __ __ __

4 Look at the picture. Complete the chart.

Name	Transportation
Yoko	*by taxi*
Ted	
Martin	
Nadia	
Sam	
Katia	

Check your answers. See page 134.

Writing

1 Look at the map. Write the words.

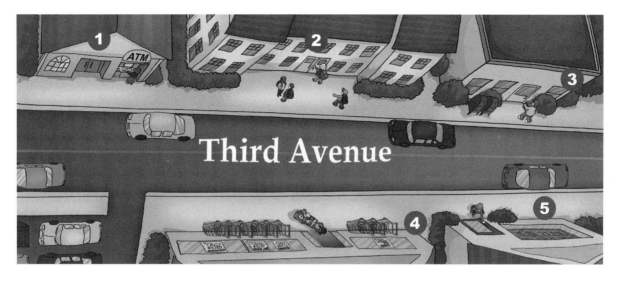

| bank | library | post office | school | supermarket |

1. _____*bank*_____   4. _____

2. _____   5. _____

3. _____

2 Look at the map in Exercise 1. Complete the sentences.

City Adult School

The City Adult School is on _____*Third Avenue*_____ . It is
                                    1

across from a _____ . The school is between
                    2

the _____ and the _____ .
        3   4

A _____ is on Third Avenue, too.
        5

Check your answers. See page 134.

3 Look at the map. Complete the sentences.

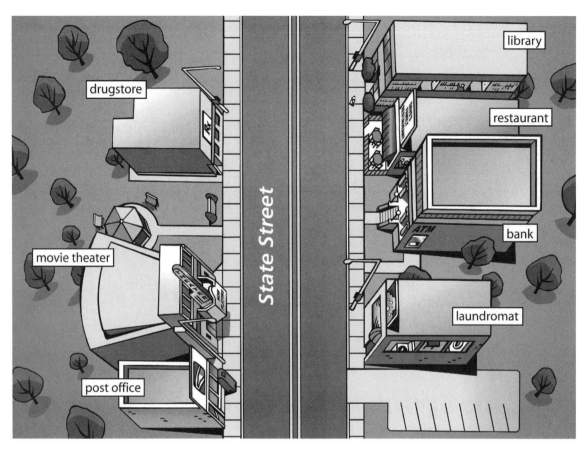

across from	between	on	next to	across from	on

STATE STREET MOVIE THEATER

The movie theater is _____*on*_____ State Street.
                        1

It is _____ a post office. A laundromat is
        2

_____ the movie theater.
        3

Dave's Family Restaurant is _____ State Street, too.
                                    4

It is _____ the library and the bank. The restaurant is
        5

_____ the drugstore. See you at the movies!
        6

Check your answers. See page 134.

1 Read the sentences. Look at the invitation. Circle the answers.

COME TO A PARTY

Where? At Binh's house
When? At 8:00 p.m. on Saturday

Binh's house is on Center Street. It is between the library and the post office. Binh's house is across from the supermarket. There is a senior center next to the supermarket, too. The address is 259 Center Street.

1. Binh's house is ___ .
   a. on Center Street
   b. on Post Street

2. Binh's house is ___ .
   a. between the senior center and the supermarket
   b. between the library and the post office

3. The supermarket is ___ .
   a. next to Binh's house
   b. across from Binh's house

4. The library is ___ .
   a. next to the post office
   b. next to Binh's house

5. The senior center is ___ .
   a. next to the supermarket
   b. across from the supermarket

Check your answers. See page 134.

2 Circle the words.

1. **bus**   b a n k (b u s) s t r e e t c a r
2. **taxi**   t r a i n f o o t t a x i b a n k
3. **train**   t a x i b u s t r a i n c e n t e r
4. **bicycle**   l i b r a r y b i c y c l e f o o t
5. **foot**   c a r a c r o s s f o o t t a x i
6. **car**   s h o p s t o r e c a r p o s t

3 Complete the conversations.

Excuse me	Next to the drugstore	Thanks	Where's the supermarket

1. **A** _Excuse me_____ . Where's the laundromat?
   B On Maple Street.
   A Thanks.

2. **A** Excuse me. Where's the senior center?
   B Across from Rosa's Restaurant.
   A _____ .

3. **A** Excuse me. _____ ?
   B Between the bank and the library.
   A Thanks.

4. **A** Excuse me. Where's the bank?
   B _____ .
   A Thanks.

Check your answers. See page 134.

Time

1 Match.

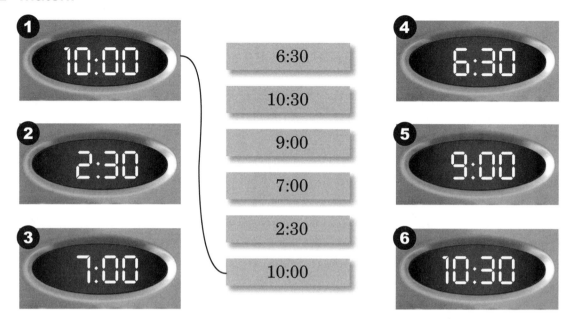

2 Read. Write the time.

①			
TIME CARD			
DAY	DATE	TIME IN	
Monday	May 12	2:30	

2:30

②			
TIME CARD			
DAY	DATE	TIME IN	
Thursday	March 3	9:00	

_____

③			
TIME CARD			
DAY	DATE	TIME IN	
Saturday	June 21	10:30	

_____

④			
TIME CARD			
DAY	DATE	TIME IN	
Tuesday	July 8	7:00	

_____

Check your answers. See page 134.

3 Look at the pictures. Write the answers.

1

A What time is it?
B It's ____9:00____ .

2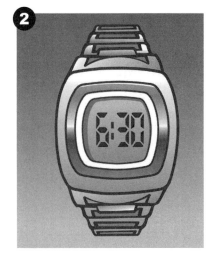

A What time is it?
B It's _____ .

3

A What time is it?
B It's _____ .

4

A What time is it?
B It's _____ .

5

A What time is it?
B It's _____ .

6

A What time is it?
B It's _____ .

Check your answers. See page 134.

Lesson B Events

1 Read. Write the answers.

1. **A** What time is the appointment?
   B At _____4:30_____ on
   _____Monday_____ .

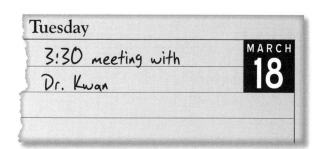

Monday
4:30 appointment with
Dr. Jones
MARCH 17

2. **A** What time is the meeting?
   B At _____ on
   _____ .

Tuesday
3:30 meeting with
Dr. Kwan
MARCH 18

3. **A** What time is the movie?
   B At _____ on
   _____ .

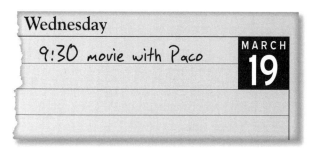

Wednesday
9:30 movie with Paco
MARCH 19

4. **A** What time is the class?
   B At _____ on
   _____ .

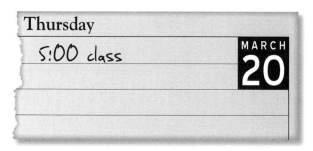

Thursday
5:00 class
MARCH 20

2 Complete the words.

appointment	class	meeting	movie	party	program

1. c _l_ _a_ _s_ _s_   4. m __ __ __ __ __ __
2. m __ __ __ __   5. a __ __ __ __ __ __ __ __ __ __ __
3. p __ __ __ __   6. p __ __ __ __ __ __

Check your answers. See page 134.

3 Look at the pictures. Write the words.

appointment	class	meeting	movie	party	program

1

A What time is the

_____*meeting*_____ ?

B At _____*10:00*_____ .

2

A What time is the

_____ ?

B At _____ .

3

A What time is the

_____ ?

B At _____ .

4

A What time is the

_____ ?

B At _____ .

5

JACK AND JANE
7:30

A What time is the

_____ ?

B At _____ .

6

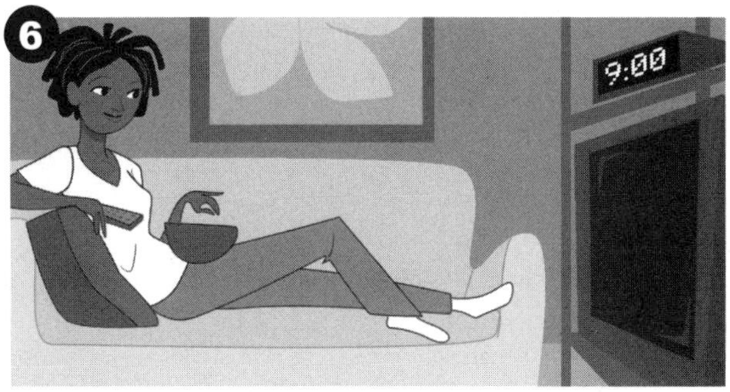

A What time is the

_____ ?

B At _____ .

Check your answers. See page 134.

Lesson C *Is your class at 11:00?*

Study the chart on page 126.

1 Look at the pictures. Write the answers.

1

From: walker@cambridge.org

To: jones@cambridge.org

Dear Employees:

Our meeting is today at 11:00 a.m.

A Is the meeting at 12:00?

B *No, it isn't*   .

2

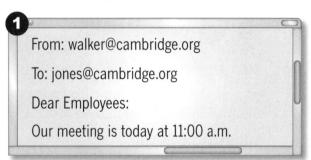

ADMIT ONE

Love at Sunset

7:45 p.m.   Sat. 8/9/08
Theater 2

A Is the movie at 8:00?

B _____ .

3

PARTY TONIGHT!

The Jam Club
Free Admission
8:30 p.m.

A Is the party at 8:30?

B _____ .

4

CITY LIGHTS
ORCHESTRA

JULY
19
SAT.

Seat K32

8:00 p.m.

A Is the concert at 6:30?

B _____ .

5

Appointment Card

Your appointment:
3:30 p.m.
September 12

A Is the appointment at 3:30?

B _____ .

Check your answers. See page 134.

2 Read. Circle the answers.

Monday, September 15			
8:30	Class	4:00	
9:00		5:00	Doctor's appointment 😧
10:00		6:30	
11:00		7:00	Movie with Louis
12:00	Lunch with Don 😊	8:00	
1:00		9:00	Birthday party 😊
2:00		10:00	
3:00	Meeting at work 😧	11:00	

1. Is the class at 8:00?   Yes, it is.   (No, it isn't.)
2. Is the appointment at 3:00?   Yes, it is.   No, it isn't.
3. Is the party at 9:00?   Yes, it is.   No, it isn't.
4. Is the movie at 6:30?   Yes, it is.   No, it isn't.
5. Is the meeting at 3:00?   Yes, it is.   No, it isn't.

3 Look at the information in Exercise 2. Match.

1. appointment   seven
2. meeting   eight-thirty
3. movie   five
4. party   three
5. class   nine

Check your answers. See page 134.

1 Read. Number the sentences in the correct order.

Mahmoud's Day

Mahmoud is busy today. His favorite TV program is at 7:30 in the morning. His doctor's appointment is at 10:30. His meeting with Abram is at 12:00. His English class is at 1:00. His concert is at 5:00. His sister's birthday party is at 8:00. What a day!

ADMIT ONE

LIVE Jazz

5:00 P.M.
SEAT 42C

LIVE JAZZ
5:00 P.M. SEAT 42C

ADMIT ONE

FROM THE DESK OF YOUR DOCTOR:

YOUR APPOINTMENT IS AT:
10:30 A.M.

Ventures

___ His sister's birthday party is at 8:00.

___ His doctor's appointment is at 10:30.

_1_ His favorite TV program is at 7:30.

___ His concert is at 5:00.

___ His English class is at 1:00.

___ His meeting with Abram is at 12:00.

2 Look at the story in Exercise 1. Write the answers.

1. What time is Mahmoud's appointment? _____*At 10:30*_____ .

2. What time is Mahmoud's meeting with Abram? _____ .

3. What time is Mahmoud's English class? _____ .

4. What time is Mahmoud's TV program? _____ .

5. What time is Mahmoud's concert? _____ .

6. What time is his sister's birthday party? _____ .

Check your answers. See page 134.

3 Match. Write the letter.

1. _d_ 8:00 a.m.   a. in the evening
2. ___ 12:00 p.m.   b. in the afternoon
3. ___ 3:30 p.m.   c. at night
4. ___ 12:00 a.m.   d. in the morning
5. ___ 7:30 p.m.   e. at noon
6. ___ 11:00 p.m.   f. at midnight

4 Match.

a. in the evening   b. in the morning   c. at night   d. in the afternoon

5 Write the words.

at midnight	at night	at noon
in the afternoon	in the evening	in the morning

1. 6:30 a.m.   _in the morning_
2. 2:00 p.m.   _____
3. 10:30 p.m.   _____
4. 12:00 p.m.   _____
5. 6:00 p.m.   _____
6. 12:00 a.m.   _____

Check your answers. See page 134.

Writing

1 Read. Complete the sentences.

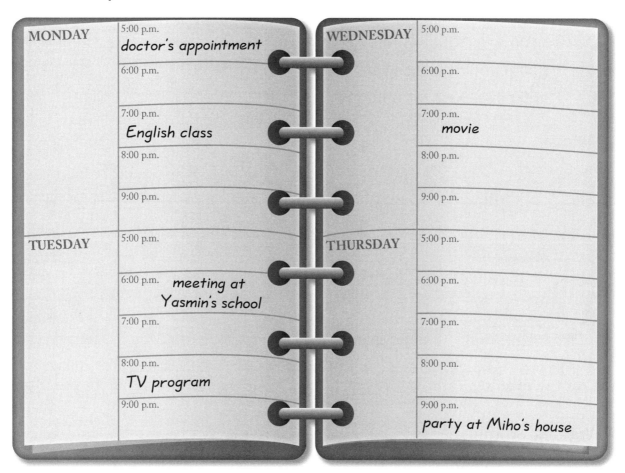

1. **A** What time is the _____ *party* _____ ?
   B At 9:00 on Thursday.

2. **A** What time is the doctor's _____ ?
   B At 5:00 on Monday.

3. **A** What time is the TV _____ ?
   B At 8:00 on Tuesday.

4. **A** What time is the English _____ ?
   B At 7:00 on Monday.

5. **A** What time is the _____ ?
   B At 7:00 on Wednesday.

6. **A** What time is the _____ ?
   B At 6:00 on Tuesday.

Check your answers. See page 135.

2 Read. Complete the story.

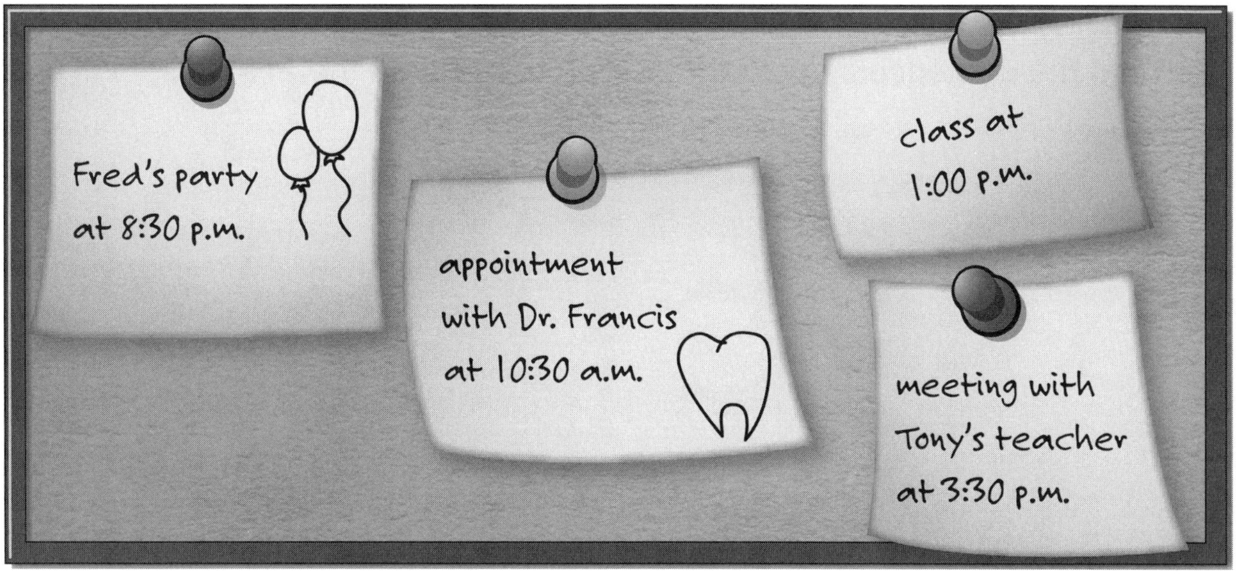

Fred's party at 8:30 p.m.

appointment with Dr. Francis at 10:30 a.m.

class at 1:00 p.m.

meeting with Tony's teacher at 3:30 p.m.

Jill is very busy today. Her _____*appointment*_____ with

Dr. Francis is at 10:30. Her _____ is at 1:00. Her
2

meeting with Tony's teacher is at _____ . Fred's
3

party is at _____ in the evening.
4

3 Complete the memo. Use the story in Exercise 2.

memo

Time: **Event:**

10:30   _____*appointment*_____

_____   _____

_____   _____

_____   _____

Check your answers. See page 135.

1 Read the sentences. Look at the invitation. Circle the answers.

1. It's a party for ___ .
   a. students and teachers
   b. Alfonso Carillo

2. This party is on ___ .
   a. Saturday
   b. Sunday

3. The party is at ___ .
   a. 8:00 a.m.
   b. 8:00 p.m.

4. The party is ___ .
   a. in the evening
   b. in the morning

Check your answers. See page 135.

2 Use the code. Write the words.

Code						
1=a	5=e	9=i	13=m	17=q	21=u	25=y
2=b	6=f	10=j	14=n	18=r	22=v	26=z
3=c	7=g	11=k	15=o	19=s	23=w	
4=d	8=h	12=l	16=p	20=t	24=x	

1. 16   1   18   20   25
   _p_ _a_ _r_ _t_ _y_

2. 3   12   1   19   19
   __   __   __   __   __

3. 5   22   5   14   9   14   7
   __   __   __   __   __   __   __

4. 13   15   18   14   9   14   7
   __   __   __   __   __   __   __

5. 13   9   4   14   9   7   8   20
   __   __   __   __   __   __   __   __

3 Find the words from Exercise 2.

m	e	l	a	p	p	o	n	o	b	o	m
i	n	t	e	v	e	n	i	n	g	f	o
p	a	r	t	y	l	i	s	h	z	a	v
i	n	g	w	e	n	c	l	a	s	s	p
g	m	o	r	n	i	n	g	i	n	o	r
c	o	n	c	m	i	d	n	i	g	h	t

Check your answers. See page 135.

 *Get ready*

Shopping

1 Look at the pictures. Match.

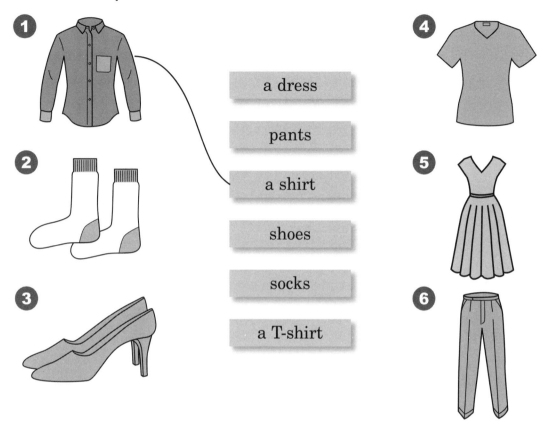

1

2

3

a dress

pants

a shirt

shoes

socks

a T-shirt

4

5

6

2 Look at the picture. Write the words.

a dress	pants	a shirt	shoes	socks	a T-shirt

1. _____a shirt_____

2. _____

3. _____

4. _____

5. _____

6. _____

BUS STOP

1

2

3

4

5

6

Check your answers. See page 135.

3 Unscramble the letters. Write the words.

dress	pants	shirt	shoes	socks	T-shirt

1. sesoh ___*shoes*___
2. rsiht ______________
3. rdses ______________
4. tapns ______________
5. koscs ______________
6. tirTsh ______________

4 Complete the puzzle. Use the words from Exercise 3.

Across →

5 

6 

Down ↓

1 

2 

3 

4 

Check your answers. See page 135.

Clothing

1 Complete the words.

blouse	jacket	raincoat	skirt	sweater	tie

1. a _t_ i e

2. a s w __ __ t e r

3. a s k __ __ t

4. a j a c k __ __

5. a r __ __ n c o a t

6. a b l __ __ s e

2 Complete the sentences. Use the words from Exercise 1.

1. The _____raincoat_____ is $49.95.

2. The _____ is $24.95.

3. The _____ is $59.95.

4. The _____ is $19.99.

5. The _____ is $19.95.

6. The _____ is $32.00.

Check your answers. See page 135.

3 Read. Write the words and the prices.

Clothing for your family . . .

$42.50

$29.99

$39.50

ON SALE NOW!

$25.99

$65.00

$24.50

1. The tie is _____ *$25.99* _____ .
2. The _____ is $39.50.
3. The sweater is _____ .
4. The _____ is $29.99.
5. The skirt is _____ .
6. The _____ is $65.00.

Check your answers. See page 135.

How much are the shoes?

1 Circle the answers.

1. How much are the ___ ?
   a. socks
   b. blouse

2. How much is the ___ ?
   a. shoes
   b. skirt

3. How much are the ___ ?
   a. tie
   b. pants

4. How much is the ___ ?
   a. raincoat
   b. socks

5. How much are the ___ ?
   a. shoes
   b. sweater

6. How much is the ___ ?
   a. shoes
   b. T-shirt

2 Write *is* or *are*.

1. **A** How much _____is_____ the tie?
   B $25.00.

2. **A** How much _____ the socks?
   B $1.99.

3. **A** How much _____ the blouse?
   B $29.99.

4. **A** How much _____ the pants?
   B $19.99.

5. **A** How much _____ the shoes?
   B $39.90.

6. **A** How much _____ the sweater?
   B $34.95.

Check your answers. See page 135.

3 Look at the picture. Write *is* or *are* and the prices.

1. **A** How much _____*is*_____ the skirt?

   B $27.50_____ .

2. **A** How much _____ the pants?

   B _____ .

3. **A** How much _____ the socks?

   B _____ .

4. **A** How much _____ the shirt?

   B _____ .

5. **A** How much _____ the sweater?

   B _____ .

6. **A** How much _____ the blouse?

   B _____ .

Check your answers. See page 135.

1 Read. Circle the answers.

From: teacher@elementary.org
To: stern@cup.org
Subject: school clothing

Dear Mrs. Stern:

The first day of school is September 9.

Your son, Billy, needs a white shirt for school. He needs a blue tie. He needs blue pants. He needs black shoes and black socks, too.

Best wishes,
Mrs. Kramer

1. Billy needs brown shoes.   Yes   No
2. Billy needs black socks.   Yes   No
3. Billy needs a blue tie.   Yes   No
4. Billy needs blue pants.   Yes   No
5. Billy needs a blue shirt.   Yes   No

2 What color is the clothing in Exercise 1? Write the words.

pants   shirt   shoes   socks   tie

white	blue	black
shirt		

Check your answers. See page 135.

3 Look at the chart. Write the answers.

Name	red	yellow	green	black	white	brown	blue
Sharmin			blouse	skirt			
Walter			tie	pants	shirt		
Hong		dress		shoes			
Omar	jacket					pants	sweater
Dora					blouse	shoes	skirt
Antonio	T-shirt	raincoat			socks		

1. **A** What color are Walter's pants?
   B _Black_ .

2. **A** What color is Hong's dress?
   B _____ .

3. **A** What color is Antonio's T-shirt?
   B _____ .

4. **A** What color is Dora's blouse?
   B _____ .

5. **A** What color is Sharmin's skirt?
   B _____ .

6. **A** What color are Dora's shoes?
   B _____ .

7. **A** What color is Omar's sweater?
   B _____ .

8. **A** What color is Walter's tie?
   B _____ .

Check your answers. See page 135.

Writing

1 Complete the words.

1. _b_ _l_ o u s e   4. t i __
2. r a i n c __ __ t   5. s w e a t __ __
3. j a __ __ e t   6. s k __ r t

2 Look at the pictures. Write the words.

1

a _____*blouse*_____

2

a _____

3

a _____

4

a _____

5

a _____

6
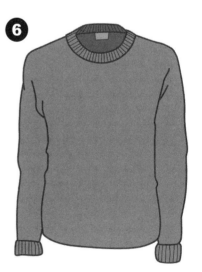
a _____

Check your answers. See page 135.

3 Complete the chart.

blouse	dress	jacket	pants	raincoat
shoes	skirt	socks	sweater	tie

Men's clothes	Men's and women's clothes	Women's clothes
	jacket	

4 Read. Complete the shopping list.

Francesca is shopping today. Her family needs new clothes. Her mother, Carmela, needs a dress. Her husband, Mario, needs a shirt. Her son, Jerome, needs pants. Her daughter, Lisa, needs a raincoat. And Francesca needs new shoes.

Francesca's Shopping List

Name	Clothing
Francesca	shoes
Lisa	_____
Jerome	_____
Carmela	_____
Mario	_____

Check your answers. See page 135.

1 Look at the picture. Complete the receipt.

Sales Receipt

The House of Clothes

32 Park Street
New York, NY 10013
(212) 555-7736

Clothing

_____tie_____ $18.00

_____ $30.00

_____ $35.00

_____ $40.00

Subtotal: . . . . _____

Tax: $5.00

Total: . . . . _____

Check your answers. See page 135.

2 Find the words.

black	blue	brown	green	orange
pink	purple	red	yellow	white

s	w	e	s	h	o	j	a	c	r
p	r	i	n	g	r	e	e	n	d
t	e	c	y	e	l	l	o	w	g
k	a	t	h	r	e	d	l	n	o
b	l	a	c	k	m	b	l	u	e
c	o	l	s	c	h	o	b	l	u
s	h	a	w	h	i	t	e	r	o
a	i	n	c	t	s	h	i	b	l
n	m	p	b	r	o	w	n	e	c
r	o	r	a	n	g	e	s	o	c
p	i	n	k	d	r	e	p	a	s
o	u	s	e	p	u	r	p	l	e

3 What is different? Cross it out.

1. shirt	blouse	~~pants~~
2. jacket	shoes	raincoat
3. shoes	T-shirt	socks
4. skirt	dress	pants
5. blouse	tie	dress

Check your answers. See page 136.

1 Complete the words.

1. m e c h a n _i_ _c_
2. w a i t __ __
3. s a l e s p e r __ __ __
4. r e c e p t i o n __ __ __
5. c u s t o d __ __ __
6. c a s h __ __ __

2 Find the words from Exercise 1.

t	r	c	a	m	n	i	v	z	q	u	i
s	a	l	e	s	p	e	r	s	o	n	t
e	c	t	r	o	k	j	u	m	g	l	u
p	t	o	w	a	i	t	e	r	t	u	h
c	a	s	h	i	e	r	e	n	o	s	l
l	i	e	s	t	w	a	p	s	h	e	a
r	e	c	e	p	t	i	o	n	i	s	t
r	o	n	p	e	c	i	k	m	a	r	r
c	c	u	s	t	o	d	i	a	n	t	e
i	e	u	z	t	i	o	n	w	a	i	z
k	m	e	c	h	a	n	i	c	g	o	s

Check your answers. See page 136.

3 Look at the pictures. Write the words.

cashier	custodian	mechanic
receptionist	salesperson	waiter

1

Fatima

receptionist

2

Edward

_____

3

Gabriel

_____

4

Cecilia

_____

5

Bruno

_____

6

Cathy

_____

4 Match.

1. Fatima   mechanic
2. Cecilia   cashier
3. Bruno   receptionist
4. Gabriel   custodian
5. Cathy   waiter
6. Edward   salesperson

Check your answers. See page 136.

Lesson B *Job duties*

1 Check (✓) the job duties.

Jobs	Sells clothes	Cleans buildings	Serves food	Answers the phone	Counts money	Fixes cars
waiter			✓			
mechanic						
salesperson						
receptionist						
custodian						
cashier						

2 Write the job duties.

| answers the phone | cleans buildings | counts money |
| fixes cars | sells clothes | serves food |

1. A waiter _____*serves food*_____ .
2. A receptionist _____ .
3. A cashier _____ .
4. A salesperson _____ .
5. A custodian _____ .
6. A mechanic _____ .

3 Write the job duties.

_____*fixes cars*_____

_____

_____

Check your answers. See page 136.

4 Look at the pictures. Write the answers.

A What does she do?

B She ___*sells clothes*___ .

A What does he do?

B He _____ .

A What does she do?

B She _____ .

A What does he do?

B He _____ .

A What does she do?

B She _____ .

A What does he do?

B He _____ .

Check your answers. See page 136.

Work **93**

Does he sell clothes?

Study the chart on page 127.

1 Look at the pictures. Circle the answers.

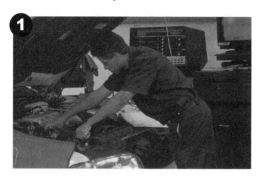

Does he fix cars?
(a.) Yes, he does.
b. No, he doesn't.

Does she answer the phone?
a. Yes, she does.
b. No, she doesn't.

Does he clean buildings?
a. Yes, he does.
b. No, he doesn't.

Does she count money?
a. Yes, she does.
b. No, she doesn't.

Does he serve food?
a. Yes, he does.
b. No, he doesn't.

Does she sell clothes?
a. Yes, she does.
b. No, she doesn't.

Check your answers. See page 136.

2 Look at the picture. Complete the sentences.

| Naoko | Juan | Imelda | Franco | Soo Yeun | Kevin |

1. **A** _Does_ Naoko _serve_ food?
   B Yes, she _does_ .

2. **A** _____ Juan _____ money?
   B Yes, he _____ .

3. **A** _____ Imelda _____ the phone?
   B No, she _____ .

4. **A** _____ Franco _____ buildings?
   B Yes, he _____ .

5. **A** _____ Soo Yeun _____ cars?
   B No, she _____ .

6. **A** _____ Kevin _____ clothes?
   B Yes, he _____ .

Check your answers. See page 136.

1 Read the letter. Complete the sentences.

Dear Mom,

I have good news! The children have jobs for the summer. In the morning, Nicolas is a mechanic. He fixes cars. In the evening, he is a waiter. He serves food. Lydia is a teacher's aide in the morning. She helps the teacher. In the evening, she is a salesperson. She sells clothes. In the afternoon, I am a receptionist. I answer the phone. Our whole family is very busy!

How are you? I miss you.

Love,
Tanya

1. **A** What does Lydia do in the evening?
   B She _____ *sells clothes* _____ .
   She is a _____ *salesperson* _____ .

2. **A** What does Nicolas do in the morning?
   B He _____ .
   He is a _____ .

3. **A** What does Lydia do in the morning?
   B She _____ .
   She is a _____ .

4. **A** What does Nicolas do in the evening?
   B He _____ .
   He is a _____ .

5. **A** What does Tanya do in the afternoon?
   B She _____ .
   She is a _____ .

Check your answers. See page 136.

2 Look at the pictures. Complete the sentences.

bus driver	housewife	painter
plumber	teacher's aide	truck driver

1

A What does he do?
B He's a ____truck driver____ .

2

A What does she do?
B She's a _____ .

3

A What does he do?
B He's a _____ .

4

A What does she do?
B She's a _____ .

5

A What does he do?
B He's a _____ .

6

A What does she do?
B She's a _____ .

Check your answers. See page 136.

1 Match.

1. sells   food
2. counts   buildings
3. serves   money
4. fixes   clothes
5. cleans   cars

2 Write the words.

buildings	bus	cars	clothes	food	money	phone

1. salesperson: sells _____*clothes*_____
2. waiter: serves _____
3. custodian: cleans _____
4. cashier: counts _____
5. mechanic: fixes _____
6. bus driver: drives a _____
7. receptionist: answers the _____

3 Look at the pictures. Complete the sentences.

She is a

_____ .

She cleans

_____*buildings*_____ .

He is a

_____ .

He counts

_____ .

She is a

_____ .

She drives

_____ .

Check your answers. See page 136.

4 Look at the pictures. Complete the letter.

Dear Aunt Rose,

How are you? We are all busy and happy. We have new jobs! Levon is a _____waiter_____ at a restaurant on
1

State Street. He _____
2

food. Tamar is a _____ .
3

She _____ a bus.
4

And I am a _____ .
5

I _____ clothes.
6

Write soon.

Love,
Rita

Check your answers. See page 136.

Another view

1 Read the sentences. Look at the ads. Circle the answers.

1. Job 1 is for a ___ .
   a. waiter
   b. plumber

2. Job 2 is for a ___ .
   a. truck driver
   b. receptionist

3. For Job 3, call ___ .
   a. 555-8743
   b. 555-3370

4. For Job 2, call ___ .
   a. 555-8743
   b. 555-2192

5. Job 4 is ___ .
   a. in the morning
   b. in the evening

6. Job 1 is ___ .
   a. in the morning
   b. in the evening

Check your answers. See page 136.

2 Write the words.

bus driver   cashier   mechanic   painter   plumber   waiter

_m_ _e_ _c_ h _a_ _n_ _i_ _c_
      o
  __ u __   __ __ __ __ __
      s
__ __ __ m __ e __
      w __ __ __ __ __
  __ __ i __ __ __ __
      f
__ __ s __ __ e __

3 Look at the chart. Complete the sentences.

	drives a bus	counts money	fixes cars	drives a truck
Ted	✓			
Jessica				✓
Rashid			✓	
Irene		✓		

1. A What's Ted's job?
  B He is a _____ *bus driver* _____ .
  A What does he do?
  B He _____ *drives a bus* _____ .

2. A What's Irene's job?
  B She is a _____ .
  A What does she do?
  B She _____ .

3. A What's Rashid's job?
  B He is a _____ .
  A What does he do?
  B He _____ .

4. A What's Jessica's job?
  B She is a _____ .
  A What does she do?
  B She _____ .

Check your answers. See page 136.

Get ready

1 Write the words.

bed	dishes	homework	laundry	dishes	lunch

1. washing the   *d i s h e s*
2. doing   __ __ __ __ __ __ __ __
3. making   __ __ __ __ __
4. doing the   __ __ __ __ __ __ __
5. making the   __ __ __
6. drying the   __ __ __ __ __ __

2 Circle the words. Then write.

1. _____*washing*_____ the dishes
   (washing) making
2. _____ lunch
   making   drying
3. _____ homework
   doing   washing
4. _____ the dishes
   drying   making
5. _____ the bed
   making   drying
6. _____ the laundry
   making   doing

3 Look at the pictures. Write the words.

making lunch

_____

_____

Check your answers. See page 137.

4 Look at the picture. Write the words.

| doing homework | doing the laundry | drying the dishes |
| making lunch | making the bed | washing the dishes |

1. _____*making the bed*_____

2. _____

3. _____

4. _____

5. _____

6. _____

Check your answers. See page 137.

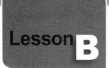
Lesson B *Outside chores*

Study the chart on page 127.

1 Look at the picture. Circle the chores.

1. taking out the trash   (cutting the grass)
2. cutting the grass   taking out the trash
3. getting the mail   walking the dog
4. walking the dog   cutting the grass
5. watering the grass   walking the dog
6. getting the mail   washing the car

Check your answers. See page 137.

2 Look at the pictures. Write the words.

Cutting	Getting	Taking out	Walking	Washing	Watering

1

A What is she doing?

B _Watering_ the grass.

2

A What is he doing?

B _____ the grass.

3

A What is she doing?

B _____ the mail.

4

A What is he doing?

B _____ the car.

5

A What is she doing?

B _____ the trash.

6

A What is he doing?

B _____ the dog.

Check your answers. See page 137.

What are they doing?

Study the chart on page 127.

1 Match.

1. drying   the bed
2. making   the trash
3. getting   the laundry
4. taking out   the dishes
5. washing   the dog
6. doing   the grass
7. cutting   the car
8. walking   the mail

2 Circle the answers. Then write.

1. **A** What _____*are*_____ they doing?
         is (are)

   B Getting the _____*mail*_____ .
         trash (mail)

2. **A** What _____ he doing?
         is   are

   B Making _____ .
         dinner   laundry

3. **A** What _____ she doing?
         is   are

   B Cutting the _____ .
         dishes   grass

4. **A** What _____ they doing?
         is   are

   B Drying the _____ .
         trash   dishes

5. **A** What _____ he doing?
         is   are

   B Walking the _____ .
         dog   laundry

6. **A** What _____ she doing?
         is   are

   B Taking out the _____ .
         trash   grass

Check your answers. See page 137.

3 Look at the pictures. Complete the sentences.

1

A What _____*is*_____ she doing?
B *Making*_____ the bed.

2

A What _____ they doing?
B _____ lunch.

3

A What _____ she doing?
B _____ the mail.

4

A What _____ they doing?
B _____ the laundry.

5

A What _____ she doing?
B _____ the dishes.

6

A What _____ he doing?
B _____ out the trash.

Check your answers. See page 137.

1 Read. Circle the answers.

> The Gomez family is busy this morning. Bonita is watering the grass. Ramon is cutting the grass. Manuel and Leon are washing the car. Luisa is taking out the trash. Magda is getting the mail.

1. Bonita is taking out the trash.   Yes   (No)
2. Luisa is getting the mail.   Yes   No
3. Magda is watering the grass.   Yes   No
4. Manuel and Leon are washing the car.   Yes   No
5. Ramon is cutting the grass.   Yes   No

2 Complete the sentences.

1. What are Manuel and Leon doing?
   They are _____*washing the car*_____ .

2. What is Bonita doing?
   She is _____ .

3. What is Ramon doing?
   He is _____ .

4. What is Magda doing?
   She is _____ .

5. What is Luisa doing?
   She is _____ .

Check your answers. See page 137.

3 Look at the pictures. Write the words.

bathroom	bedroom	dining room
kitchen	laundry room	living room

1

bathroom

2

_____

3

_____

4

_____

5

_____

6

_____

4 Circle the rooms.

Chores	Room	
1. drying the dishes	laundry room	(kitchen)
2. making the bed	bedroom	bathroom
3. washing the dishes	kitchen	bedroom
4. doing the laundry	living room	laundry room
5. making lunch	kitchen	bathroom

Check your answers. See page 137.

1 Complete the words.

1. d _r_ _y_ _i_ _n_ _g_   the dishes
2. w __ __ __ __ __ __   the dishes
3. m __ __ __ __ __   lunch
4. d __ __ __ __   homework
5. m __ __ __ __ __   the bed
6. d __ __ __ __   the laundry

2 Read. Write the chores.

Chore	Sun	Min	Dae	Chul	Soo	Chin
do homework	✓					
make the bed			✓			
make lunch				✓		
wash the dishes						✓
dry the dishes					✓	
do the laundry		✓				

1. Sun is _____doing homework_____ .
2. Dae is _____ .
3. Soo is _____ .
4. Chin is _____ .
5. Min is _____ .
6. Chul is _____ .

Check your answers. See page 137.

110 Unit 9

3 Look at the picture. Complete the chore chart.

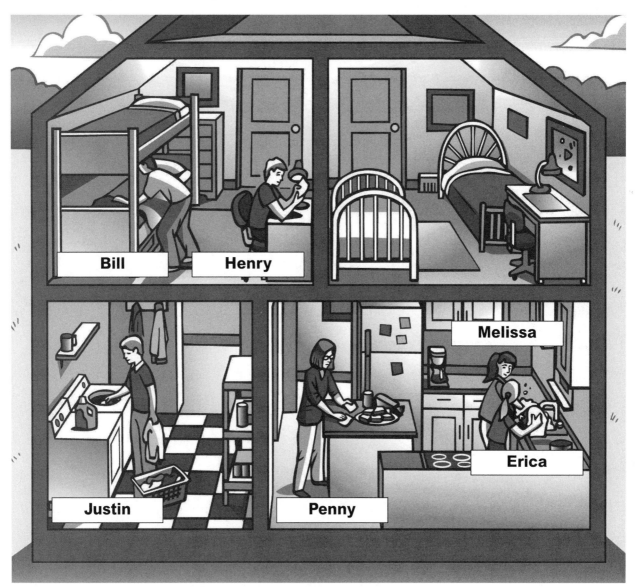

Name	Chore
Justin	*do the laundry*
Melissa	
Henry	
Penny	
Bill	
Erica	

Check your answers. See page 137.

1 Read the sentences. Look at the calendar. Circle the answers.

Monday	Tuesday	Wednesday	Thursday	Friday
Erin	**Adam**	**Andy**	**Suzy**	**Sara**
make the bed	cut the grass	wash the car	do the laundry	take out the trash

1. Today is Wednesday. Andy is ___ .
   a. making the bed
   (b.) washing the car

2. Today is Monday. Erin is ___ .
   a. making the bed
   b. taking out the trash

3. Today is Thursday. Suzy is ___ .
   a. cutting the grass
   b. doing the laundry

4. Today is Tuesday. Adam is ___ .
   a. washing the car
   b. cutting the grass

5. Today is Friday. Sara is ___ .
   a. taking out the trash
   b. doing the laundry

Check your answers. See page 137.

2 Unscramble the letters. Write the words.

bathroom	bedroom	dining room
kitchen	laundry room	living room

1. b t h a o o r m   _bathroom_
2. r o m o b d e   _____
3. k c h n e t i   _____
4. n d i g n i   o r o m   _____
5. v i n g l i   m o r o   _____
6. y r d u n l a   m r o o   _____

3 Write the rooms.

1. making lunch   _kitchen_
2. doing the laundry   _____
3. drying the dishes   _____
4. making the bed   _____
5. washing the dishes   _____

4 Complete the chart.

cutting the grass	drying the dishes	making lunch
making the bed	walking the dog	washing the car
washing the dishes	watering the grass	

Chores inside the house	Chores outside the house
drying the dishes	cutting the grass

Check your answers. See page 137.

Leisure

Get ready

1 Complete the words.

1. f _i_ s h
2. s w ___ m
3. d ___ n c e
4. e x ___ ___ c i s e
5. p l a y   c ___ ___ d s
6. p l ___ ___   b a s k ___ ___ b a l l

2 Find the words.

| basketball | cards | dance | exercise | fish | play | swim |

b	i	c	y	t	a	b	l	s	h
p	d	a	n	c	e	y	z	f	i
e	x	e	r	p	l	a	y	m	b
e	x	e	r	c	i	s	e	d	o
c	a	r	d	s	m	o	n	w	t
e	y	f	i	s	w	i	m	y	a
d	a	v	n	g	e	l	u	s	w
n	c	f	i	s	h	i	m	b	a
b	a	s	k	e	t	b	a	l	l
d	s	z	o	n	f	r	e	x	p

Check your answers. See page 137.

3 Look at the picture. Write the words.

exercise	fish	play basketball	play cards	swim

1. *play basketball*

2. _____

3. _____

4. _____

5. _____

Check your answers. See page 138.

Around the house

Study the chart on page 127.

1 Match. Then write the words.

1. read — in the garden   _____ *read magazines* _____
2. play — TV   _____
3. listen to — the guitar   _____
4. watch — magazines   _____
5. work — music   _____

2 Look at the pictures. Write the words.

1. **A** What does she like to do?
   B Listen to _____ *music* _____ .

2. **A** What does he like to do?
   B Watch _____ *to TV* _____ .

3. **A** What does she like to do?
   B Play _____ *to the guitar* _____ .

4. **A** What does he like to do?
   B Work _____ *to the garden* _____ .

5. **A** What does she like to do?
   B Read _____ *to magazines* _____ .

Check your answers. See page 138.

3 Look at the picture. Write the words.

Cook	Listen to music	Play the guitar
Read magazines	Watch TV	Work in the garden

1. What does Sarita like to do?   *Cook* .
2. What does Steve like to do?   .
3. What does Lola like to do?   .
4. What does Marco like to do?   .
5. What does Kaitlin like to do?   .
6. What does Dennis like to do?   .

Check your answers. See page 138.

Study the chart on page 127.

1 Write *like* or *likes*.

1. **A** What does she like to do?
   B She _____*likes*_____ to work in the garden.

2. **A** What does he like to do?
   B He _____ to play the guitar.

3. **A** What do they like to do?
   B They _____ to watch TV.

4. **A** What does she like to do?
   B She _____ to read magazines.

5. **A** What do they like to do?
   B They _____ to play cards.

6. **A** What do you like to do?
   B I _____ to cook.

7. **A** What does she like to do?
   B She _____ to play basketball.

8. **A** What do you like to do?
   B I _____ to play soccer.

Check your answers. See page 138.

2 Look at the pictures. Circle *like* or *likes*. Complete the sentences.

1

A What does he like to do?

B He _____*likes*_____
    like ⟨likes⟩

to _____*exercise*_____ .

2

A What does she like to do?

B She _____
    like   likes

to _____ .

3

A What do they like to do?

B They _____
    like   likes

to _____ .

4

A What does he like to do?

B He _____
    like   likes

to _____ .

5

A What do they like to do?

B They _____
    like   likes

to _____ .

6

A What does she like to do?

B She _____
    like   likes

to _____ .

Check your answers. See page 138.

1 Look at the Web site. Circle the answers.

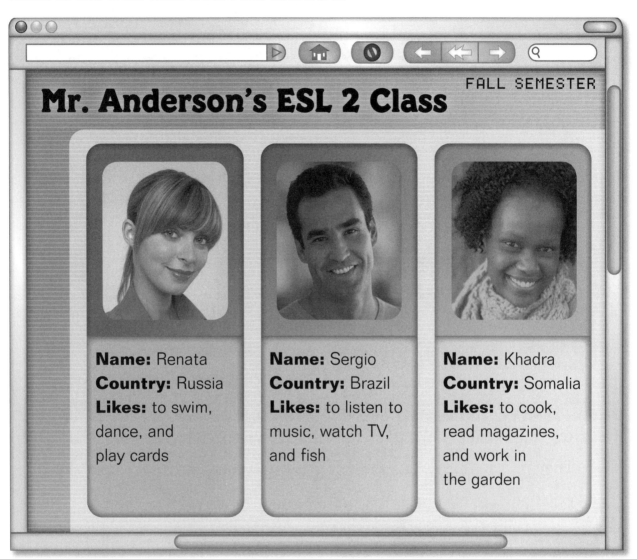

FALL SEMESTER

Mr. Anderson's ESL 2 Class

Name: Renata
Country: Russia
Likes: to swim, dance, and play cards

Name: Sergio
Country: Brazil
Likes: to listen to music, watch TV, and fish

Name: Khadra
Country: Somalia
Likes: to cook, read magazines, and work in the garden

1. Renata likes to swim.	(Yes)	No
2. Sergio likes to cook.	Yes	No
3. Khadra likes to play cards.	Yes	No
4. Renata likes to work in the garden.	Yes	No
5. Sergio likes to watch TV.	Yes	No
6. Khadra likes to read magazines.	Yes	No

Check your answers. See page 138.

2 Look at the pictures. What do they like to do? Match.

travel

shop

volunteer

exercise

go to the movies

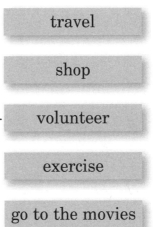

Check your answers. See page 138.

Lesson E Writing

1 Complete the words.

| cook | dance | fish | shop | swim | volunteer |

1. _s_ _w_ _i_ m
2. ___ ___ ___ h
3. ___ ___ ___ k
4. ___ ___ ___ p
5. ___ ___ ___ ___ e
6. ___ ___ ___ ___ ___ ___ ___ ___ r

2 Read. Complete the sentences.

	work in the garden	fish	volunteer	play cards	swim
Flor	✓				
Alvaro				✓	
Vera					✓
Brian		✓			
Kim			✓		

1. Flor likes to _____ *work in the garden* _____ .
2. Vera likes to _____ .
3. Kim likes to _____ .
4. Brian likes to _____ .
5. Alvaro likes to _____ .

Check your answers. See page 138.

3 Complete the sentences.

exercise	go	listen to	play	read	visit	watch

1. Jason likes to _____exercise_____ on Monday.
2. Jason likes to _____ TV on Thursday.
3. Jason likes to _____ magazines on Wednesday.
4. Jason likes to _____ to the movies on Sunday.
5. Jason likes to _____ friends on Friday.
6. Jason likes to _____ basketball on Saturday.
7. Jason likes to _____ music on Tuesday.

4 Write the information from Exercise 3 on the calendar.

Jason's Calendar

Sunday	Monday	Tuesday	Wednesday	Thursday	Friday	Saturday
1	2	3	4	5	6	7
_____	*exercise*	_____	_____	_____	_____	_____
_____	_____	_____	_____	_____	_____	_____

Check your answers. See page 138.

1 Read the sentences. Look at the catalog. Circle the answers.

Community Center Classes
September 2 to December 12

Learn to dance!
Monday and Wednesday
11:00 a.m. – 12:30 p.m.
Room 110
$95.00

Learn to swim!
Tuesday and Thursday
9:00 a.m. – 10:30 a.m.
Pool
$100.00

Learn to play basketball!
Friday
2:30 p.m. – 4:30 p.m.
Room 115
$75.00

Learn to cook!
Monday and Wednesday
10:30 a.m. – 12:00 p.m.
Room 121
$85.00

1. The dance class is in Room ___ .
   (a.) 110
   b. 115

2. The cooking class is in Room ___ .
   a. 115
   b. 121

3. The basketball class is ___ .
   a. in the morning
   b. in the afternoon

4. The swimming class is ___ .
   a. in the morning
   b. in the evening

5. The dance class is ___ .
   a. $85.00
   b. $95.00

6. The basketball class is ___ .
   a. $75.00
   b. $100.00

Check your answers. See page 138.

2 Unscramble the letters. Write the words.

| listen to music | play basketball | play cards |
| play the guitar | read magazines | visit friends |

1. y a p l   d s a r c   *play cards*
2. s i t v i   f i r n e s d
3. a y l p   e h t   t r a i u g
4. a e d r   g z a m n i e a s
5. l y a p   k b l s e t a a l b
6. n e t s l i   o t   c s i u m

3 Complete the chart.

| go to the movies   run   shop   travel   visit friends   volunteer |

Costs money $$$	No money ~~$$$~~
travel	

4 Complete the chart.

dance	go to the movies	listen to music	play basketball
play cards	play soccer	read magazines	run
swim	watch TV		

Exercise	No exercise
dance	

Check your answers. See page 138.

Reference

Possessive adjectives

Questions

What's	my his her its our your their	phone number?

Answers

My Your His Her Its Our Your Their	phone number is 555-3348.

Simple present of *have*

Yes / No questions

Do	I	
Do	you	
Does	he	
Does	she	have a laundry room?
Does	it	
Do	we	
Do	you	
Do	they	

Short answers

Yes,	I	do.
	you	do.
	he	does.
	she	does.
	it	does.
	we	do.
	you	do.
	they	do.

No,	I	don't.
	you	don't.
	he	doesn't.
	she	doesn't.
	it	doesn't.
	we	don't.
	you	don't.
	they	don't.

don't = do not
doesn't = does not

Present of *be*

Yes / No questions

Am	I	
Are	you	
Is	he	
Is	she	from Somalia?
Is	it	
Are	we	
Are	you	
Are	they	

Short answers

Yes,	I	am.
	you	are.
	he	is.
	she	is.
	it	is.
	we	are.
	you	are.
	they	are.

No,	I'm not.
	you aren't.
	he isn't.
	she isn't.
	it isn't.
	we aren't.
	you aren't.
	they aren't.

I'm = I am
You're = You are
They're = They are

He's = He is
She's = She is

It's = It is
We're = We are

aren't = are not
isn't = is not

Present continuous

Questions with *What*

What	am	I	doing?
	are	you	
	is	he	
	is	she	
	is	it	
	are	we	
	are	you	
	are	they	

Short answers

Working.

Simple present of *like to* + verb

Questions with *What*

What	do	I	like to do?
	do	you	
	does	he	
	does	she	
	does	it	
	do	we	
	do	you	
	do	they	

Answers

I	like	to swim.
You	like	
He	likes	
She	likes	
It	likes	
You	like	
We	like	
They	like	

Yes / No questions

Do	I	like to swim?
Do	you	
Does	he	
Does	she	
Does	it	
Do	we	
Do	you	
Do	they	

Short answers

Yes,	I	do.	No,	I	don't.
	you	do.		you	don't.
	he	does.		he	doesn't.
	she	does.		she	doesn't.
	it	does.		it	doesn't.
	we	do.		we	don't.
	you	do.		you	don't.
	they	do.		they	don't.

Cardinal numbers

0 zero	12 twelve	24 twenty-four	36 thirty-six
1 one	13 thirteen	25 twenty-five	37 thirty-seven
2 two	14 fourteen	26 twenty-six	38 thirty-eight
3 three	15 fifteen	27 twenty-seven	39 thirty-nine
4 four	16 sixteen	28 twenty-eight	40 forty
5 five	17 seventeen	29 twenty-nine	50 fifty
6 six	18 eighteen	30 thirty	60 sixty
7 seven	19 nineteen	31 thirty-one	70 seventy
8 eight	20 twenty	32 thirty-two	80 eighty
9 nine	21 twenty-one	33 thirty-three	90 ninety
10 ten	22 twenty-two	34 thirty-four	100 one hundred
11 eleven	23 twenty-three	35 thirty-five	1,000 one thousand

Ordinal numbers

1st first	9th ninth	17th seventeenth	25th twenty-fifth
2nd second	10th tenth	18th eighteenth	26th twenty-sixth
3rd third	11th eleventh	19th nineteenth	27th twenty-seventh
4th fourth	12th twelfth	20th twentieth	28th twenty-eighth
5th fifth	13th thirteenth	21st twenty-first	29th twenty-ninth
6th sixth	14th fourteenth	22nd twenty-second	30th thirtieth
7th seventh	15th fifteenth	23rd twenty-third	31st thirty-first
8th eighth	16th sixteenth	24th twenty-fourth	

Metric equivalents

1 inch = 25 millimeters	1 dry ounce = 28 grams	1 fluid ounce = 30 milliliters
1 foot = 30 centimeters	1 pound = .45 kilograms	1 quart = .95 liters
1 yard = .9 meters	1 mile = 1.6 kilometers	1 gallon = 3.8 liters

Converting Fahrenheit temperatures to Celsius

Subtract 30 and divide by 2:   80°F = approximately 25°C

Countries and nationalities

Afghanistan	Afghan	Georgia	Georgian	Poland	Polish
Albania	Albanian	Germany	German	Portugal	Portuguese
Algeria	Algerian	Ghana	Ghanaian	Puerto Rico	Puerto Rican
Angola	Angolan	Greece	Greek	Republic of the Congo	Congolese
Argentina	Argentine	Grenada	Grenadian		
Armenia	Armenian	Guatemala	Guatemalan	Romania	Romanian
Australia	Australian	Guyana	Guyanese	Russia	Russian
Austria	Austrian	Haiti	Haitian	Saudi Arabia	Saudi
Azerbaijan	Azerbaijani	Herzegovina	Herzegovinian	Senegal	Senegalese
Bahamas	Bahamian	Honduras	Honduran	Serbia	Serbian
Bahrain	Bahraini	Hungary	Hungarian	Sierra Leone	Sierra Leonean
Bangladesh	Bangladeshi	India	Indian	Singapore	Singaporean
Barbados	Barbadian	Indonesia	Indonesian	Slovakia	Slovak
Belarus	Belarussian	Iran	Iranian	Somalia	Somali
Belgium	Belgian	Iraq	Iraqi	South Africa	South African
Belize	Belizean	Ireland	Irish	South Korea	Korean
Benin	Beninese	Israel	Israeli	Spain	Spanish
Bolivia	Bolivian	Italy	Italian	Sri Lanka	Sri Lankan
Bosnia	Bosnian	Jamaica	Jamaican	Sudan	Sudanese
Brazil	Brazilian	Japan	Japanese	Sweden	Swedish
Bulgaria	Bulgarian	Jordan	Jordanian	Switzerland	Swiss
Cambodia	Cambodian	Kazakhstan	Kazakhstani	Syria	Syrian
Cameroon	Cameroonian	Kenya	Kenyan	Tajikistan	Tajikistani
Canada	Canadian	Kuwait	Kuwaiti	Tanzania	Tanzanian
Cape Verde	Cape Verdean	Laos	Laotian	Thailand	Thai
Chile	Chilean	Lebanon	Lebanese	Togo	Togolese
China	Chinese	Liberia	Liberian	Tonga	Tongan
Colombia	Colombian	Lithuania	Lithuanian	Trinidad	Trinidadian
Comoros	Comoran	Macedonia	Macedonian	Tunisia	Tunisian
Costa Rica	Costa Rican	Malaysia	Malaysian	Turkey	Turkish
Côte d'Ivoire	Ivoirian	Mexico	Mexican	Turkmenistan	Turkmen
Croatia	Croatian	Moldova	Moldovan	Uganda	Ugandan
Cuba	Cuban	Morocco	Moroccan	Ukraine	Ukrainian
Dominica	Dominican	Nepal	Nepali	United Arab Emirates	Emirati
Dominican Republic	Dominican	Netherlands	Dutch		
		New Zealand	New Zealander	United Kingdom	British
Ecuador	Ecuadorian	Nicaragua	Nicaraguan		
Egypt	Egyptian	Niger	Nigerien	United States	American
El Salvador	Salvadoran	Nigeria	Nigerian	Uruguay	Uruguayan
Equatorial Guinea	Equatorial Guinean	Norway	Norwegian	Uzbekistan	Uzbekistani
		Pakistan	Pakistani	Venezuela	Venezuelan
Eritrea	Eritrean	Panama	Panamanian	Vietnam	Vietnamese
Ethiopia	Ethiopian	Paraguay	Paraguayan	Yemen	Yemeni
Fiji	Fijian	Peru	Peruvian	Zambia	Zambian
France	French	Philippines	Filipino	Zimbabwe	Zimbabwean

Answer key

Welcome

Exercise 1 page 2

D, H, L, P, T, X

Exercise 2 page 2

c, f, i, l, o, r, u, x

Exercise 3 page 3

1. W, Write   4. L, Listen
2. P, Point   5. C, Circle
3. R, Read   6. M, Match

Exercise 4 page 4

1, 4, 7, 10, 13, 16, 19

Exercise 5 page 4

one, three, five, seven, nine,
twelve, fourteen, sixteen,
eighteen, twenty

Exercise 6 page 5

1. one   5. two
2. four   6. five
3. three   7. six
4. eight   8. seven

Unit 1: Personal information

Lesson A: Get ready

Exercise 1 page 6

1. first name
2. last name
3. country
4. area code
5. phone number

Exercise 2 page 6

1. Anna
2. Lopez
3. Mexico
4. 254
5. 555-2992

Exercise 3 page 7

1. last name
2. first name
3. phone number
4. area code
5. ID card

Exercise 4 page 7

1. phone number
2. area code

3. last name
4. first name

Exercise 5 page 7

1. first name
2. last name
3. area code
4. phone number

Lesson B: Countries

Exercise 1 page 8

1. f   2. a   3. e   4. c   5. b   6. d

Exercise 2 page 8

1. China
2. Brazil
3. Russia
4. Mexico
5. Somalia

Exercise 3 page 9

1. Somalia
2. The United States
3. China
4. Brazil
5. Russia
6. Mexico

Lesson C: What's your name?

Exercise 1 page 10

1. her   5. her
2. his   6. his
3. his   7. her
4. her   8. his

Exercise 2 page 11

1. your   5. your
2. My   6. My
3. your   7. your
4. My   8. My

Exercise 3 page 11

1. Manuel
2. Alvez
3. 917
4. 555-9845

Lesson D: Reading

Exercise 1 page 12

1. Boris Egorov
2. Egorov
3. Boris
4. Russia

Exercise 2 page 12

1. c   2. a   3. d   4. b

Exercise 3 page 13

February, March, May, June,
August, September, November

Exercise 4 page 13

1. In June
2. In January
3. In February
4. In April
5. In July

Lesson E: Writing

Exercise 1 page 14

1. country
2. area code
3. first name
4. last name
5. phone number

Exercise 2 page 14

1. first name
2. last name
3. area code
4. phone number
5. China

Exercise 3 page 15

1. Emma
2. Harris
3. 407
4. 555-6524

Exercise 4 page 15

First name: Octavio
Last name: Diaz
Birthday: December 7, 1990
Country: Mexico
Area code: 206
Phone number: 555-3687

Lesson F: Another view

Exercise 1 page 16

1. b
2. b
3. a
4. a
5. b
6. b

130

Exercise 2 page 17

1. c o (c o u n t r y) t e
2. m e (n a m e) a n
3. l J u l (J u n e) J y
4. m o n (m o n t h) t h
5. d a y (b i r t h d a y) b i
6. p h (p h o n e) p n

Exercise 3 page 17

1. August   5. Russia
2. 555-9832   6. January
3. 972   7. Brazil
4. Somalia

Exercise 4 page 17

1: January   12: December
4: April   3: March
8: August   2: February
7: July   10: October
5: May   9: September
11: November   6: June

Unit 2: At school

Lesson A: Get ready

Exercise 1 page 18

1. a chair
2. a notebook
3. a desk
4. a book
5. a computer

Exercise 2 page 19

a notebook, a chair, a desk

Exercise 3 page 19

1. book   4. computer
2. notebook   5. pencil
3. desk   6. chair

Lesson B: Classroom objects

Exercise 1 page 20

1. stapler
2. ruler
3. dictionary
4. eraser
5. paper

Exercise 2 page 20

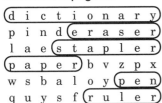

(d i c t i o n a r y)
p i n d (e r a s e r)
l a e (s t a p l e r)
(p a p e r) b v z p x
w s b a l o y (p e n)
q u y s f (r u l e r)

Exercise 3 page 21

1. dictionary   4. ruler
2. paper   5. stapler
3. pen   6. eraser

Exercise 4 page 21

1. pen   4. dictionary
2. stapler   5. ruler
3. eraser   6. paper

Lesson C: Where's my pencil?

Exercise 1 page 22

1. c   2. e   3. a   4. b   5. d

Exercise 2 page 22

1. In
2. On
3. On
4. On
5. On

Exercise 3 page 23

1. On the desk
2. In the notebook
3. In the desk
4. On the floor
5. On the desk
6. On the chair

Lesson D: Reading

Exercise 1 page 24

1. n o t (n o t e b o o k) t e
2. e r (e r a s e r) a s
3. c (c o m p u t e r) t e r
4. e n (p e n c i l) i l p
5. e s k (d e s k) d e n c i l
6. k o b o o o k (b o o k)

Exercise 2 page 24

1. You need a dictionary.
2. You need a pencil.
3. You need a notebook.
4. You need a ruler.
5. You need an eraser.

Exercise 3 page 25

1: Monday
2: Tuesday
3: Wednesday
4: Thursday
5: Friday
6: Saturday
7: Sunday

Exercise 4 page 25

           S u n d a y
   M o n d a y
         t
    T u e s d a y
    F r i d a y
   W e d n e s d a y
         a
T h u r s d a y

Exercise 5 page 25

1. Friday
2. Thursday
3. Tuesday

Lesson E: Writing

Exercise 1 page 26

1. notebook   4. eraser
2. dictionary   5. pencil
3. ruler

Exercise 2 page 27

1. on   4. in
2. on   5. on
3. on   6. in

Exercise 3 page 27

1. pencil   4. paper
2. eraser   5. dictionary
3. ruler   6. notebook

Exercise 4 page 27

1. pencil   4. paper
2. eraser   5. dictionary
3. ruler   6. notebook

Lesson F: Another view

Exercise 1 page 28

1. b   2. b   3. a   4. b   5. a

Exercise 2 page 29

Across

1. pen
4. dictionary
5. ruler
7. eraser
8. desk

Down

2. notebook
3. stapler
6. pencil

Unit 3: Friends and family

Lesson A: Get ready

Exercise 1 page 30

1. grandmother
2. daughter
3. grandfather
4. mother
5. father
6. son

Exercise 2 page 30

1. son
2. father
3. mother
4. grandmother
5. daughter
6. grandfather

Exercise 3 page 31

father, grandfather, daughter, grandmother, mother

Exercise 4 page 31

1. father
2. mother
3. grandmother
4. grandfather
5. daughter

Lesson B: Family members

Exercise 1 page 32

1. sister - brother
2. son - daughter
3. grandmother - grandfather
4. husband - wife
5. mother - father
6. aunt - uncle

Exercise 2 page 32

```
              m
      b r o t h e r
  a u n t
              h u s b a n d
      w i f e
s i s t e r
```

Exercise 3 page 33

1. a
2. a
3. b

Exercise 4 page 33

1. brother
2. sister
3. father
4. mother
5. uncle

Lesson C: Do you have a sister?

Exercise 1 page 34

1. No, we don't.
2. Yes, I do.
3. Yes, we do.
4. No, I don't.
5. Yes, I do.

Exercise 2 page 35

1. sister
2. daughter
3. husband
4. son

Lesson D: Reading

Exercise 1 page 36

1. wife
2. daughter
3. father
4. mother

Exercise 2 page 36

1. No
2. Yes
3. Yes
4. No
5. No

Exercise 3 page 37

Male: boy, man
Female: girl, woman
Male or Female: baby, teenager

Exercise 4 page 37

1. woman
2. man
3. boy
4. girl
5. woman
6. man
7. woman
8. teenager
9. baby

Lesson E: Writing

Exercise 1 page 38

1. wife
2. uncle
3. sister
4. mother
5. daughter
6. grandfather

Exercise 2 page 38

1. uncle
2. sister
3. daughter
4. wife
5. mother
6. grandfather

Exercise 3 page 38

1. father
2. grandfather
3. baby
4. mother
5. grandmother

Exercise 4 page 39

1. father
2. mother
3. brother
4. wife
5. son
6. daughter

Exercise 5 page 39

1. husband
2. son
3. father
4. son
5. brother
6. father

Lesson F: Another view

Exercise 1 page 40

1. b 2. b 3. a 4. a 5. b 6. a

Exercise 2 page 41

1. father
2. aunt
3. son
4. aunt
5. brother
6. wife
7. man

Exercise 3 page 41

```
w i f e  o r d i m  b a b y  g
o  w o m a n  r s i s t r v e
s i s t e r  s t f l c e l o
c a m e r t  m o t h e r  n k
h u s b a n d  s h o u m k l
n m o w i e  t e e n a g e r
u n c l e  t b u b f w a p o
```

Unit 4: Health

Lesson A: Get ready

Exercise 1 page 42

1. patient
2. doctor's office
3. nurse
4. medicine
5. doctor
6. patient

Exercise 2 page 43

1. doctor's office
2. doctor
3. nurse
4. patient
5. medicine

Exercise 3 page 43

1. medicine
2. doctor
3. patient
4. office

Lesson B: Parts of the body

Exercise 1 page 44

1. hand
2. head
3. foot
4. arm
5. leg
6. stomach

Exercise 2 page 44

1. stomach   4. head
2. arm   5. hand
3. foot   6. leg

Exercise 3 page 45

1. foot   4. stomach
2. hand   5. leg
3. head   6. arm

Lesson C: My feet hurt.

Exercise 1 page 46

1. eye - eyes
2. hand - hands
3. foot - feet
4. arm - arms
5. leg - legs
6. head - heads

Exercise 2 page 46

```
r e p (l e g s) t u r
f q b o p (h a n d s)
o u m j (f e e t) k e
(f o o t) t l s c z j
t e r (h e a d) z y e
(a r m s) c o m u t r
l e k f t p (e y e s)
```

Exercise 3 page 47

1. eye, eyes
2. hand, hands
3. foot, feet
4. leg, legs
5. arm, arms

Exercise 4 page 47

1. legs
2. arm
3. foot
4. hands
5. eyes
6. stomach

Lesson D: Reading

Exercise 1 page 48

1. stomach   4. arm
2. hand   5. leg
3. foot   6. head

Exercise 2 page 49

1. c   2. d   3. f   4. b   5. a   6. e

Exercise 3 page 49

1. toothache
2. headache
3. cold

Lesson E: Writing

Exercise 1 page 50

Across

1. sore throat
4. arm
5. cold
7. eyes

Down

1. stomachache
2. headache
3. toothache
6. legs

Exercise 2 page 51

1. cold
2. fever
3. headache
4. stomachache
5. sore throat

Exercise 3 page 51

1. sore throat
2. cold
3. headache
4. stomachache
5. fever

Lesson F: Another view

Exercise 1 page 52

1. a   2. b   3. b   4. a   5. b

Exercise 2 page 53

1. hands
2. eyes
3. feet
4. arms
5. legs

Exercise 3 page 53

1. My head
2. My stomach
3. My leg
4. My foot

Unit 5: Around town

Lesson A: Get ready

Exercise 1 page 54

1. bank
2. library
3. restaurant
4. supermarket
5. school

Exercise 2 page 55

1. street   4. library
2. bank   5. restaurant
3. school   6. supermarket

Exercise 3 page 55

Down

1. restaurant
2. street
3. school

Across

3. supermarket
4. bank
5. library

Lesson B: Places around town

Exercise 1 page 56

1. drugstore
2. movie theater
3. senior center
4. post office

Exercise 2 page 56

```
h p o s (h o s p i t a l) i n
n o x u l f n e c e t d y g
o w e n t (d r u g s t o r e)
r e (p o s t o f f i c e) l o
c a (s e n i o r c e n t e r)
e g z x u r i s h o u m k l
n (m o v i e t h e a t e r) m
l a n o (l a u n d r o m a t)
```

Exercise 3 page 57

1. hospital   4. movie theater
2. drugstore   5. laundromat
3. post office   6. senior center

Lesson C: It's on Main Street.

Exercise 1 page 58

1. next to   4. on
2. across from   5. between
3. next to   6. across from

Exercise 2 page 59

1. Next to
2. Across from
3. Between
4. On

Exercise 3 page 59

1. c   2. d   3. a   4. e   5. b

Lesson D: Reading

Exercise 1 page 60

1. bank
2. restaurant
3. drugstore
4. hospital

Exercise 2 page 60

1. hospital
2. Lake Street
3. bank, drugstore
4. restaurant

Exercise 3 page 61

1. car   4. bus
2. taxi   5. train
3. bicycle   6. foot

Exercise 4 page 61

Yoko: by taxi
Ted: by bus
Martin: by bicycle
Nadia: by car
Sam: on foot
Katia: by train

Lesson E: Writing

Exercise 1 page 62

1. bank   4. supermarket
2. school   5. library
3. post office

Exercise 2 page 62

1. Third Avenue
2. supermarket
3. bank
4. post office
5. library

Exercise 3 page 63

1. on   4. on
2. next to   5. between
3. across from 6. across from

Lesson F: Another view

Exercise 1 page 64

1. a   2. b   3. b   4. b   5. a

Exercise 2 page 65

1. b a n k (b u s) s t r e e t c a r
2. t r a i n f o o t (t a x i) b a n k
3. t a x i b u s (t r a i n) c e n t e r
4. l i b r a r y (b i c y c l e) f o o t
5. c a r a c r o s s (f o o t) t a x i
6. s h o p s t o r e (c a r) p o s t

Exercise 3 page 65

1. Excuse me
2. Thanks
3. Where's the supermarket
4. Next to the drugstore

Unit 6: Time

Lesson A: Get ready

Exercise 1 page 66

1. 10:00   4. 6:30
2. 2:30   5. 9:00
3. 7:00   6. 10:30

Exercise 2 page 66

1. 2:30
2. 9:00
3. 10:30
4. 7:00

Exercise 3 page 67

1. 9:00   4. 10:30
2. 6:30   5. 10:00
3. 2:30   6. 7:00

Lesson B: Events

Exercise 1 page 68

1. 4:30, Monday
2. 3:30, Tuesday
3. 9:30, Wednesday
4. 5:00, Thursday

Exercise 2 page 68

1. class   4. meeting
2. movie   5. appointment
3. party   6. program

Exercise 3 page 69

1A. meeting
1B. 10:00
2A. party
2B. 8:30
3A. class
3B. 5:00
4A. appointment
4B. 3:30
5A. movie

5B. 7:30
6A. program
6B. 9:00

Lesson C: Is your class at 11:00?

Exercise 1 page 70

1. No, it isn't
2. No, it isn't
3. Yes, it is
4. No, it isn't
5. Yes, it is

Exercise 2 page 71

1. No, it isn't.
2. No, it isn't.
3. Yes, it is.
4. No, it isn't.
5. Yes, it is.

Exercise 3 page 71

1. appointment - five
2. meeting - three
3. movie - seven
4. party - nine
5. class - eight-thirty

Lesson D: Reading

Exercise 1 page 72

6: His sister's birthday party is at 8:00.
2: His doctor's appointment is at 10:30.
1: His favorite TV program is at 7:30.
5: His concert is at 5:00.
4: His English class is at 1:00.
3: His meeting with Abram is at 12:00.

Exercise 2 page 72

1. At 10:30   4. At 7:30
2. At 12:00   5. At 5:00
3. At 1:00   6. At 8:00

Exercise 3 page 73

1. d   2. e   3. b   4. f   5. a   6. c

Exercise 4 page 73

1. d   2. c   3. a   4. b

Exercise 5 page 73

1. in the morning
2. in the afternoon
3. at night

4. at noon
5. in the evening
6. at midnight

Lesson E: Writing

Exercise 1 page 74

1. party
2. appointment
3. program
4. class
5. movie
6. meeting

Exercise 2 page 75

1. appointment
2. class
3. 3:30
4. 8:30

Exercise 3 page 75

10:30 – appointment
1:00 – class
3:30 – meeting
8:30 – party

Lesson F: Another view

Exercise 1 page 76

1. a 2. a 3. b 4. a

Exercise 2 page 77

1. party
2. class
3. evening
4. morning
5. midnight

Exercise 3 page 77

```
m  e  l  a (p  p  o  n  o  b  o  m
i  n  t (e  v  e  n  i  n  g) f  o
(p  a  r  t  y) l  i  s  h  z  a  v
i  n  g  w  e  n (c  l  a  s  s) p
g (m  o  r  n  i  n  g) i  n  o  r
c  o  n  c (m  i  d  n  i  g  h  t)
```

Unit 7: Shopping

Lesson A: Get ready

Exercise 1 page 78

1. a shirt   4. a T-shirt
2. socks   5. a dress
3. shoes   6. pants

Exercise 2 page 78

1. a shirt   4. pants
2. a T-shirt   5. socks
3. a dress   6. shoes

Exercise 3 page 79

1. shoes   4. pants
2. shirt   5. socks
3. dress   6. T-shirt

Exercise 4 page 79

Down	Across
1. shoes	5. shirt
2. T-shirt	6. socks
3. pants	
4. dress	

Lesson B: Clothing

Exercise 1 page 80

1. a tie   4. a jacket
2. a sweater 5. a raincoat
3. a skirt   6. a blouse

Exercise 2 page 80

1. raincoat   4. blouse
2. skirt   5. tie
3. jacket   6. sweater

Exercise 3 page 81

1. $25.99   4. blouse
2. raincoat 5. $24.50
3. $42.50   6. jacket

Lesson C: How much are the shoes?

Exercise 1 page 82

1. a 2. b 3. b 4. a 5. a 6. b

Exercise 2 page 82

1. is   4. are
2. are   5. are
3. is   6. is

Exercise 3 page 83

1A. is   4A. is
1B. $27.50   4B. $36.50
2A. are   5A. is
2B. $45.00   5B. $35.00
3A. are   6A. is
3B. $3.50   6B. $42.00

Lesson D: Reading

Exercise 1 page 84

1. No
2. Yes
3. Yes
4. Yes
5. No

Exercise 2 page 84

white: shirt
blue: pants, tie
black: shoes, socks

Exercise 3 page 85

1. Black   5. Black
2. Yellow 6. Brown
3. Red   7. Blue
4. White   8. Green

Lesson E: Writing

Exercise 1 page 86

1. blouse   4. tie
2. raincoat 5. sweater
3. jacket   6. skirt

Exercise 2 page 86

1. blouse   4. skirt
2. tie   5. jacket
3. raincoat 6. sweater

Exercise 3 page 87

Men's clothes: tie
Men's and women's clothes:
jacket, pants, raincoat, shoes,
socks, sweater
Women's clothes: blouse, dress,
skirt

Exercise 4 page 87

Francesca: shoes
Lisa: raincoat
Jerome: pants
Carmela: dress
Mario: shirt

Lesson F: Another view

Exercise 1 page 88

Clothing
tie
shirt
pants
shoes
Subtotal: $123.00
Total: $128.00

Exercise 2 page 89

```
s w e s h o j a c r
p r i n (g r e e n) d
t e c (y e l l o w) g
k a t h (r e d) l n o
(b l a c k) m (b l u e)
c o l s c h o b l u
s h a (w h i t e) r o
a i n c t s h i b l
n m p (b r o w n) e c
r (o r a n g e) s o c
(p i n k) d r e p a s
o u s e (p u r p l e)
```

Exercise 3 page 89

1. pants   4. pants
2. shoes   5. tie
3. T-shirt

Unit 8: Work

Lesson A: Get ready

Exercise 1 page 90

1. mechanic   4. receptionist
2. waiter   5. custodian
3. salesperson   6. cashier

Exercise 2 page 90

```
t r c a m n i v z q u i
(s a l e s p e r s o n) t
e c t r o k j u m g l u
p t o (w a i t e r) t u h
(c a s h i e r) e n o s l
l i e s t w a p s h e a
(r e c e p t i o n i s t)
r o n p e c i k m a r r
c (c u s t o d i a n) t e
i e u z t i o n w a i t z
k (m e c h a n i c) g o s
```

Exercise 3 page 91

1. receptionist   4. salesperson
2. cashier   5. custodian
3. waiter   6. mechanic

Exercise 4 page 91

1. Fatima - receptionist
2. Cecilia - salesperson
3. Bruno - custodian
4. Gabriel - waiter
5. Cathy - mechanic
6. Edward - cashier

Lesson B: Job duties

Exercise 1 page 92

waiter: serves food
mechanic: fixes cars
salesperson: sells clothes
receptionist: answers the phone
custodian: cleans buildings
cashier: counts money

Exercise 2 page 92

1. serves food
2. answers the phone
3. counts money
4. sells clothes
5. cleans buildings
6. fixes cars

Exercise 3 page 92

1. fixes cars
2. sells clothes
3. serves food

Exercise 4 page 93

1. sells clothes
2. cleans buildings
3. counts money
4. serves food
5. answers the phone
6. fixes cars

Lesson C: Does he sell clothes?

Exercise 1 page 94

1. a 2. a 3. b 4. a 5. b 6. a

Exercise 2 page 95

1A. Does, serve
1B. does
2A. Does, count
2B. does
3A. Does, answer
3B. doesn't
4A. Does, clean
4B. does
5A. Does, fix
5B. doesn't
6A. Does, sell
6B. does

Lesson D: Reading

Exercise 1 page 96

1. sells clothes, salesperson
2. fixes cars, mechanic

3. helps the teacher, teacher's aide
4. serves food, waiter
5. answers the phone, receptionist

Exercise 2 page 97

1. truck driver
2. housewife
3. plumber
4. teacher's aide
5. bus driver
6. painter

Lesson E: Writing

Exercise 1 page 98

1. sells clothes
2. counts money
3. serves food
4. fixes cars
5. cleans buildings

Exercise 2 page 98

1. clothes   5. cars
2. food   6. bus
3. buildings   7. phone
4. money

Exercise 3 page 98

1. custodian, buildings
2. cashier, money
3. bus driver, a bus

Exercise 4 page 99

1. waiter   4. drives
2. serves   5. salesperson
3. bus driver   6. sell

Lesson F: Another view

Exercise 1 page 100

1. a 2. b 3. b 4. a 5. b 6. a

Exercise 2 page 101

```
m e c h a n i c
        o
    b u s   d r i v e r
        s
p l u m b e r
        w a i t e r
    p a i n t e r
        f
c a s h i e r
```

Exercise 3 page 101

1. bus driver, drives a bus
2. cashier, counts money
3. mechanic, fixes cars
4. truck driver, drives a truck

Unit 9: Daily living

Lesson A: Get ready

Exercise 1 page 102

1. dishes
2. homework
3. lunch
4. laundry
5. bed
6. dishes

Exercise 2 page 102

1. washing
2. making
3. doing
4. drying
5. making
6. doing

Exercise 3 page 102

1. making lunch
2. doing homework
3. washing the dishes

Exercise 4 page 103

1. making the bed
2. doing homework
3. doing the laundry
4. making lunch
5. washing the dishes
6. drying the dishes

Lesson B: Outside chores

Exercise 1 page 104

1. cutting the grass
2. taking out the trash
3. getting the mail
4. walking the dog
5. watering the grass
6. washing the car

Exercise 2 page 105

1. Watering
2. Cutting
3. Getting
4. Washing
5. Taking out
6. Walking

Lesson C: What are they doing?

Exercise 1 page 106

1. drying the dishes
2. making the bed
3. getting the mail
4. taking out the trash
5. washing the car

6. doing the laundry
7. cutting the grass
8. walking the dog

Exercise 2 page 106

1A. are
1B. mail
2A. is
2B. dinner
3A. is
3B. grass
4A. are
4B. dishes
5A. is
5B. dog
6A. is
6B. trash

Exercise 3 page 107

1A. is
1B. Making
2A. are
2B. Making
3A. is
3B. Getting
4A. are
4B. Doing
5A. is
5B. Washing
6A. is
6B. Taking

Lesson D: Reading

Exercise 1 page 108

1. No
2. No
3. No
4. Yes
5. Yes

Exercise 2 page 108

1. washing the car
2. watering the grass
3. cutting the grass
4. getting the mail
5. taking out the trash

Exercise 3 page 109

1. bathroom
2. bedroom
3. living room
4. laundry room
5. kitchen
6. dining room

Exercise 4 page 109

1. kitchen
2. bedroom
3. kitchen
4. laundry room
5. kitchen

Lesson E: Writing

Exercise 1 page 110

1. drying
2. washing
3. making
4. doing
5. making
6. doing

Exercise 2 page 110

1. doing homework
2. making the bed
3. drying the dishes
4. washing the dishes
5. doing the laundry
6. making lunch

Exercise 3 page 111

Justin: do the laundry
Melissa: wash the dishes
Henry: do homework
Penny: make lunch
Bill: make the bed
Erica: dry the dishes

Lesson F: Another view

Exercise 1 page 112

1. b 2. a 3. b 4. b 5. a

Exercise 2 page 113

1. bathroom
2. bedroom
3. kitchen
4. dining room
5. living room
6. laundry room

Exercise 3 page 113

1. kitchen
2. laundry room
3. kitchen
4. bedroom
5. kitchen

Exercise 4 page 113

Chores inside the house: drying the dishes, making lunch, making the bed, washing the dishes
Chores outside the house: cutting the grass, walking the dog, washing the car, watering the grass

Unit 10: Leisure

Lesson A: Get ready

Exercise 1 page 114

1. fish
2. swim
3. dance
4. exercise
5. play cards
6. play basketball

Exercise 2 page 114

```
b i c y t a b l s h
p (d a n c e) y z f i
e x e r (p l a y) m b
(e x e r c i s e) d o
(c a r d s) m o n w t
e y f i (s w i m) y a
d a v n g e l u s w
n c (f i s h) i m b a
(b a s k e t b a l l)
d s z o n f r e x p
```

Exercise 3 page 115

1. play basketball
2. exercise
3. swim
4. fish
5. play cards

Lesson B: Around the house

Exercise 1 page 116

1. read magazines
2. play the guitar
3. listen to music
4. watch TV
5. work in the garden

Exercise 2 page 116

1. music
2. TV
3. the guitar
4. in the garden
5. magazines

Exercise 3 page 117

1. Cook
2. Listen to music
3. Read magazines
4. Play the guitar
5. Work in the garden
6. Watch TV

Lesson C: I like to watch TV.

Exercise 1 page 118

1. likes   5. like
2. likes   6. like
3. like   7. likes
4. likes   8. like

Exercise 2 page 119

1. likes, exercise
2. likes, cook
3. like, swim
4. likes, fish
5. like, dance
6. likes, play cards

Lesson D: Reading

Exercise 1 page 120

1. Yes   4. No
2. No   5. Yes
3. No   6. Yes

Exercise 2 page 121

1. volunteer
2. go to the movies
3. exercise
4. travel
5. shop

Lesson E: Writing

Exercise 1 page 122

1. swim   4. shop
2. fish   5. dance
3. cook   6. volunteer

Exercise 2 page 122

1. work in the garden
2. swim
3. volunteer
4. fish
5. play cards

Exercise 3 page 123

1. exercise   5. visit
2. watch   6. play
3. read   7. listen to
4. go

Exercise 4 page 123

Sunday: go to the movies
Monday: exercise
Tuesday: listen to music
Wednesday: read magazines
Thursday: watch TV
Friday: visit friends
Saturday: play basketball

Lesson F: Another view

Exercise 1 page 124

1. a 2. b 3. b 4. a 5. b 6. a

Exercise 2 page 125

1. play cards
2. visit friends
3. play the guitar
4. read magazines
5. play basketball
6. listen to music

Exercise 3 page 125

Costs money: travel, go to the movies, shop
No money: run, visit friends, volunteer

Exercise 4 page 125

Exercise: dance, play basketball, play soccer, run, swim
No exercise: go to the movies, listen to music, play cards, read magazines, watch TV

Illustration credits

Ben Hasler: 19, 31, 39, 57, 81, 86, 99, 109

Frank Montagna: 8, 26, 44, 53, 69, 80, 91, 95, 117

John Batten: 21, 29, 36, 48, 49, 78, 98, 107, 115

Kevin Brown: 3, 22, 47, 50, 52, 59, 63, 67, 72, 73, 103, 111

Kim Johnson: 33, 38, 45, 50, 97

Paul Hampson: 20, 34, 47, 78, 85, 88, 108, 116

Phil Williams: 5, 58, 62

Scott Mooney: 23, 35, 46, 61, 104, 121

William Waitzman: 11, 27, 43, 49, 83, 92, 112

Photography credits